THE BIDDING PRAYER
for the Church's Year

THE BIDDING PRAYER

for the Church's Year

edited by
DAVID KONSTANT and PAUL BURNS

MAYHEW-McCRIMMON
Great Wakering

First published in Great Britain in 1976
Revised edition published in Great Britain in 1982 by
MAYHEW-McCRIMMON LTD
10-12 High St, Great Wakering, Essex, SS3 0EQ

ISBN 0 85597 112 6

Typeset by Carlinpoint Ltd, London
Reproduced from copy supplied,
printed and bound in Great Britain
by Billing & Sons Ltd, London & Worcester

Contents

Foreword to the Revised Edition

This collection is offered to priests and others responsible for preparing for the celebration of Mass as a guide to help them compose the Bidding Prayer for Sundays throughout the three-year cycle, for major Feastdays and certain special occasions.

The prayers have been composed by about twenty priests and lay people, and the editors would like to express their gratitude to them for their patient work in writing the prayers, as one of them expressed it, 'in the cold'. It is one thing to write prayers for a particular occasion on that occasion, and quite another to write them without the stimulus of immediacy.

For this new edition, the themes of the prayers and intentions have in the main been retained, but the expression has in many cases been modified so as to bring out the unity of the Bidding Prayer and to give greater emphasis to the congregation's priestly function, exercised in the Bidding Prayer, of praying for the needs of the Church and the world. The editors are grateful to Mgr Anthony Boylan, formerly National Adviser for Liturgical Formation to the Liturgy Commission of the Bishops' Conference of England and Wales, for his help and advice in this respect.

The hope of authors and editors is that this compilation will help priests and congregations at Mass to pray to the Lord with an ever-increasing understanding and confidence.

David Konstant
Paul Burns

Introduction

History

Bidding prayers, or the prayers of the faithful, have a long history. Their origin can probably be traced to the Jewish synagogue prayers with which the first Christians were inevitably familiar, and from which the style of these prayers seems to have developed. They were prayers of blessing, of thanksgiving and petition, and as such soon found their way into the greater prayer of the Church, the Eucharist. St Paul writes to Timothy (1 Timothy 2.1): 'My advice is that, first of all, there should be prayers offered for everyone—petitions, intercessions and thanksgiving—and especially for kings and others in authority, so that we may be able to live religious and reverent lives in peace and quiet.' We read in the Acts of the Apostles (2.42): 'These (the early Christians) remained faithful to the teaching of the apostles, to the brotherhood, to the breaking of the bread and to the prayers.' The prayers referred to here are probably those which we now call bidding prayers.

The first letter of Clement (AD 96) includes prayers of intercession for use during Mass. Justin (AD 150), in a section of the *Apology* (I, 65) concerned with the practice of Christian worship, mentions prayers for the community as the preliminary to the Eucharist: 'After thus washing him who has been persuaded and has given assent, we bring him to those that are called the brethren, where they are assembled, to offer prayers in common, both for ourselves and for him who has been illuminated and for all men everywhere, with all our hearts, that as we have learned the truth so we may also be counted worthy to be found good citizens and guardians of the commandments, that we may be saved with an eternal salvation. We salute one another with a kiss when we have ended the prayers. Then is brought to the president of the brethren bread and a cup of water and wine.' The writer of the *Didache* (a second-century document on the apostolic teaching) in speaking of the ceremonies surrounding the Eucharist says: 'Allow the prophets to give thanks as much as they will.'

Gradually the pattern and place of these prayers changed. In the fifth century Pope Gelasius moved them forward from the offertory to the beginning of Mass. In the following century, as liturgical ceremonies were gradually becoming less flexible, and as some of the intercessions were then being included in the eucharistic prayer, bidding prayers at the beginning of Mass were omitted, leaving only the *Kyrie eleison* followed by a single collect. Nonetheless, bidding prayers in the vernacular were not uncommon during the Middle Ages and survived in parts of Europe even after the Council of Trent.

The earliest form of the prayer of the faithful with which we are still familiar is the series of prayers said on Good Friday. The tradition for these prayers goes back to the fifth century or earlier. The form of the prayers is useful to note. An example will illustrate this simply.

For the unity of Christians

Let us pray
for all our brothers and sisters
who share our faith in Jesus Christ,
that God may gather and keep together in one Church
all those who seek the truth with sincerity.

(Silent prayer)

Almighty and eternal God,
you keep together those you have united.
Look kindly on all who follow Jesus your Son.
We are all consecrated to you by our common baptism;
make us one in the fulness of faith,
and keep us one in the fellowship of love.
We ask this through Christ our Lord
Amen.

The prayer begins with a fairly detailed statement of the intention, given either by a reader or the priest; there is then a pause for silent prayer by all those present; then the priest gathers these prayers together in his own, presidential prayer, to which all answer Amen.

The Constitution on the Sacred Liturgy of the second Vatican Council decreed that the prayer of the faithful should be restored: 'There is to be restored, after the Gospel with its homily, the *Community Prayer* or *Prayer of the Faithful.* By this prayer, in which the people are to take part, intercession will be made for Holy Church, for the civil authorities, for those oppressed by various needs, for all mankind, and for the salvation of the entire world' (art. 53).

Structure

The general structure laid down is very simple: an invitation to prayer by the celebrant; the petitions themselves; a pause for silent prayer; and the final prayer also said by the celebrant. Each petition ends with an invocation to which the whole congregation is invited to respond.

The pattern is thus slightly different from that of the Good Friday prayers, in that the celebrant's 'collect' prayer following each petition is omitted in favour of an invocation and response, and there is instead only one collect said by the celebrant at the end of the series of petitions.

In the *General Instruction on the Roman Missal,* issued by the Vatican as a guide to the implementation of the liturgical reforms issuing from the Council document, the following guidelines for the form of the Bidding Prayer are laid down:

> In the Prayer of the Faithful (General Intercession or Bidding Prayer) the people exercise their priestly function by praying for all mankind. It is desirable that a prayer of this type be normally included in Masses celebrated with the people, so that they may pray for Holy Church, for those in authority, for those oppressed by various needs, for all mankind and for the salvation of the entire world.
>
> The sequence of intentions is usually as follows:
> (a) for the needs of the Church;
> (b) for civil authorities and for the salvation of the whole world;
> (c) for those oppressed by any kind of need;
> (d) for the local commnity.
>
> However, on special occasions, such as in Masses conjoined with Confirmations, Weddings or Funerals, the list of intentions may be concerned more explicitly with the particular occasion.
>
> It is the function of the priest to preside over this prayer; he introduces it with a brief invitation, and concludes it with a prayer. The intention themselves are best proposed by a deacon, a cantor or some other assistant. The community as a whole expresses its prayer either by a common response after each petition, or else by a prayerful silence (GIRM, 45-6)

These guidelines were recently expanded and clarified by the Liturgical Commission for the Bishops' Conference of England and Wales in *The Parish Mass: A Resource Book for Clergy, Religious and Laity* (London, CTS, 1981), which repeats the above passage from the *General Instruction* and then goes on to say:

> The following points need to be made clear:
> — its purpose as an intercession by the Church on behalf of mankind;
> — its form: one single prayer with various intentions;
> — the place of silence in it;
> — the role of a lay reader, who proposes intentions for the people's prayer.

In offering this prayer the Church shows its responsibility to pray not only for its own needs but for those of all creation. This is its 'priestly function' which here refers to the general priesthood of laity and clergy alike. The sequence of intentions given embraces needs both spiritual and material, world-wide and local, long-standing and immediate.

The intercessions are invitations to prayer, not prayers in themselves.

They should commence with such phrases as:

We pray that...
Let us pray for...
For.. we pray to the Lord.

Each invitation should be short and easy to take in. There follows a brief silence for all to think about the intention.

Then the intentions may be taken up by a prayer and response such as 'Lord, hear us. Lord, graciously hear us', 'Lord, in your mercy. Hear our prayer'.

Before the final prayer by the priest it is customary in England and Wales to say the 'Hail Mary' or some other invocation to our Lady.

Each of the points made here can be expanded a little further and related to the prayers collected in this book, so as to enable those who use it to appreciate the principles underlying the composition of the prayers — which it is hoped will be followed by those composing their own 'intentions', either on the basis of the themes suggested or on other topics.

Purpose

The concept of an intercession by the Church on behalf of mankind, when related to the local parish community gathered to celebrate the Sunday Eucharist (the typical situation for which this book caters), means that the prayer is outward-looking rather than inward-looking. The parish is praying as the local Church on behalf of the wider community and in doing so, as is stated, is exercising its priestly function. This general principle does not exclude intentions expressed on behalf of those in immediate situations of need, on behalf of members of the parish or the locality, but the general principle is that the faithful gathered in one place should be praying not for themselves, but for others. This, after all, is the basic orientation of Christian life.

In a book designed for general use, it is of course not possible to suggest themes relating to local needs, except in general terms.

These will have to be supplied by each parish, but care needs to be taken to preserve the concept of prayer going from the community gathered together to pray for those outside it, rather than the community praying for itself. The Collect prayer at the beginning of Mass, the prayer over the offerings and the prayer after communion are usually in the form of prayers for the needs of the community, with the celebrant there exercising *his* priestly function of offering the prayer on behalf of the faithful. The orientation of the Bidding Prayer, which is the prayer *of* the faithful, not *for* the faithful, needs to be different. Otherwise there is a danger of the whole eucharistic celebration becoming introverted in character. Christ gave himself that the world might be saved, and it is the duty of his followers to follow his example, not to turn his sacrifice back on him: 'This is the love I mean: not our love for God, but God's love for us when he sent his Son to be the sacrifice that takes our sins away. My dear people, since God has loved us so much, we too should love one another. No one has ever seen God, but as long as we love one another God will live in us and his love will be complete in us' (1 John 3. 11-12).

This would seem to express the essence of what the Bidding Prayer should be about. The new commandment is one and indivisible. We are commanded to love God *and* our neighbour, but since we cannot see God, the only way we can express our love of God is through practical love of our neighbour. So we pray essentially not for ourselves but for others, and 'others' in the widest sense. That certain man still goes down from Jerusalem to Jericho every day all over the world: we see pictures of him on television lying mutilated by the road-side in Guatemala and El Salvador; he sits with a begging bowl in Calcutta; he stands in the dole queues nearer home. He is the victim of the sin of the world which Christ came to take away, which we pray may be taken away. Christ's work needs to be completed everywhere, every day, and we, the Church, are praying that with the help of the Spirit (which is *promised* to us, only we sometimes don't know how to find it), we may be the agents of its completion.

Even once this basic orientation *ad extra* is understood, however, there would seem to be two major pitfalls to be avoided in prayers of petition. The first is that in seeming to pray for others, we are really praying for ourselvs. So, for example, if we give out as an intention: 'That we who receive unconditional love from God, may give the same sort of love for others...', this would appear to fulfil the essence of the principle contained in the passage from 1 John quoted above, but it is really a prayer for *us*, not for others: 'That *we* may give...' It asks for a moral quality to become present in us, one to which no objection could be raised in itself, but one which, in context of the priestly function we are here exercising, we should be desiring for others. But if the wording is simply changed to: 'As all receive unconditional love from God, we pray that they may give the same sort of love...', then the intention becomes directly for others, for 'all'. To take another example: if we announce that, 'We pray for the gift of making sensible decisions, that when we have to choose we will choose what is best', we may mean (and probably do) 'what is best for others, for our neighbour, for the world', so the sentiment expressed is unexceptionable, but the form of expression asks for a quality to be given to *us*. But if we say: 'We pray that all Christians may possess the great gift of discernment, so that when they have to make choices, they will choose what is best', then the desired benefit for others, for the world, is the same, but we are praying 'for all Christians', not just for us, ourselves gathered in one particular church. (The revisions made to this second edition have been made with this distinction in mind, and it is one that needs to be thought of carefully when completing the suggested 'intentions' that follow the biddings set out in full.)

The second pitfall is the perennial temptation to revert to Paganism, to appeal to God as Jupiter, as the *deus ex machina* who will resolve all problems on his own if only we petition him hard and often enough. Of course, when it is put as crudely as that, we will all plead 'not guilty'. We are not, after all, praying for riches, benefits, 'favours' for ourselves, as the Pagans did (do?). But even when we pray for undeniably Christian intentions, we can still pray for them in a pagan way, if we are not careful (and it is in fact far easier to compose pagan prayers than Christian ones!). We can still suggest that somehow it is God's fault that things are wrong with the world, that he is somehow witholding his favours simply because of his inscrutable will which somehow we have to influence by importuning him till he carries out what we ask of him. It is, for example, perfectly justifiable for Christians to desire better industrial relations (and where more so than in Britain in the 1980's?). But if we announce an intention, 'for better industrial relations, that workers and managers may come to understand each other's problems and work for a common aim', while the *intention* is Christian, the expression is Pagan, because what we are suggesting, if we are not careful, is that we want a heavenly conciliation service to come down and sort the whole thing out. The Christian prayer, in the context, would be rather: 'For workers and managers in industry, that they may come to understand one another's problems and work for a common aim'. Here we are praying for the *people* concerned, that God's will may come about in and through them, not for the *thing,* that God will do it instead of us, because we can't. Without him, maybe we can't but without us he can't either, because that is not how he works. In prayers of petition, it is vital never to lose sight of the Incarnation, of the fact that the Christian God is not 'out there', but became man and showed us how to live as men and women. His kingdom is where the blind see, the lame walk and the poor have the good news brought to them, not a palace on Mount Olympus.

Form

'One single prayer with various intentions': so it is 'The Bidding Prayer', not a series of bidding prayers. Within that one prayer there are parts, but these should not become separate prayers in themselves. The opening invitation by the celebrant should not be in a form which addresses itself directly to God. So in this book the invitation generally announces the theme based on the readings for the day and invites the faithful to pray for the 'needs' of the Church and the world related to that theme. Without being too rigid about it, there is an attempt at a unity of content as well as of form.

The individual biddings are invitations to prayer, not prayers in themselves. So they should never start: 'Lord, we pray...', 'Father, we ask...' etc., as this would make them prayers in themselves, but rather 'Let us pray for...', 'We pray that...', which are announcements of intention to pray. The 'prayer and response' which follow the brief pause after each invitation to pray are perhaps better thought of as just the response to the invitation to 'pray for' contained in each bidding. So they should not introduce separate subjects of their own, or the unity of the Bidding Prayer is lost. The same is true if new themes are introduced to the preamble to the invocation of Our Lady or the invitation to silent prayer.

The place of silence

Rather, the 'places' of silence, because the structure of bidding and response becomes illogical if there is no pause for silent prayer between the invitation to pray and the response, the spoken request that the prayer be heard. The prayer is made silently in the pause by each person present, otherwise there is no prayer we can ask to be heard. It can be just a moment's pause for thought, but has an essential place in the structure of invitation-prayer-response. The pause for silent prayer after the specific invitation to do so should be somewhat longer, a chance to reflect on all the intentions announced and other needs that suggest themselves to each one of us.

The role of a lay reader

Again, or 'readers', as there is no reason (except perhaps considerations of space) why each bidding should not be given out by a different person. Indeed this can be a most effective vehicle for giving expression to the fact that this is the prayer of the faithful. One or more lay readers there should certainly be: if the celebrant 'takes' the biddings as well as his opening invitation he is in a sense accepting his own invitation, which is hardly generous. On the other hand, it is his function, and his alone, as president of the assembly, to issue the invitation to the faithful at the opening of the Bidding Prayer and to close it with a concluding prayer, which 'collects' the various intentions and offers them directly to the Father, and this presidential function should not be delegated to other members of the congregation.

Composition of the Bidding Prayer

This is intended as a source book, not as a substitute for what should be a rewarding task for members of the parish. The guidelines in *The Parish Mass* on this point state that: 'The actual composition is undertaken by the priest, the parish liturgy committee, or any suitable group within the parish. Some parishes have found it useful to have a box at the church entrance in which individual petitions may be placed.' Obviously it depends on the individual parish, though one would hope that the first option would not be a permanent one in any parish. If individual petitions are to be placed in a box, it might be as well to have some form of instruction/discussion about the general principles underlying the purpose and form of the Bidding Prayer before the practice is adopted, and, at least for a time, to look at the petitions and make any necessary amendments before reading them out.

Because of the general function of the Bidding Prayer as a prayer of the community for the Church and the world, most of the themes and biddings in this book are fairly general, partly from necessity, and partly because of the general principle that the Prayer should be outward-looking, not inward-looking. But the Liturgical Commission does go on to say that, 'More specific intercessions may be composed for special celebrations such as weddings, funerals, house Masses, children's Masses, etc.' There is a final section in this book of Bidding Prayers for such occasions as weddings and funerals, which should perhaps be regarded rather more as a source of ideas on which more specific words can be based.

It is, surely, important to see the Bidding Prayer as an integral part of the liturgy, not as a break from it into personal concerns. For this reason, a certain formality of language has been retained in the prayer suggested here. The subject of religious language is one for endless debate, but the compilers have tried to provide texts that measure up to the level of language used in the rest of the eucharistic liturgy, not to lapse into more colloquial speech, which can be as off-putting to some as it can be involving to others. Again, this is not a matter for dogmatic decision-making, but a thought to bear in mind when composing prayers suitable for the parish and the occasion. Obviously, in smaller and less formal gatherings, a less formal style is more appropriate.

There is a set of prayers for each Sunday of the three-year cycle, for the major feasts and for a few special occasions. Each set gives the invitation to prayer by the celebrant, two biddings in full, with the responses, three suggested themes for further biddings (printed in italic), invitations to the invocation of Our Lady and to silent prayer, and the celebrant's concluding prayer. The pattern varies slightly in a few cases. One or both of the biddings given in full draw on the readings of the day, so as to contribute to a unified eucharistic celebration. The suggestions for the three other biddings are to remind the celebrant and those preparing the Mass of what the community may need to pray for, without intending to impose too much on the relevance that should also be sought — within the general consideration of an outgoing Prayer.

Several variations of invocation and response after each bidding are used. Again, further variation is possible, but remembering that these are basically requests that the prayer be heard, not new prayers in themselves. It is suggested that the invocation and response to be used are printed in the parish newsletter, or announced before the biddings, or, of course, both. Some attention can perhaps be paid, without being too pedantic, to the grammatical link between the bidding and the invocation and response. For example, if the bidding uses the form 'For...' it needs to end either with 'we pray to the Lord' or a similar phrase, if the usual invocation and response 'Lord, hear us. Lord, graciously hear us' is used; otherwise there is, as far the words are concerned, nothing to hear.

'Ask, and it will be given to you; search and you will find; knock and the door will be opened to you. For the one who asks will receive; the one who searches always finds; the one who knocks will always have the door opened to him' (Matthew 7. 7-8) This is the scriptural basis for the prayer of petition. But it works because God has already given everything, because the door is always open. We have to find out what to take, where to look, and then learn to give in our turn, to be the open door to others.

1st SUNDAY IN ORDINARY TIME

The Baptism of Our Lord

Celebrant We are all baptised sons and daughters of the Father and can call Jesus our brother. With our brother, let us approach the Father in familiarity and trust to pray for the needs of the whole human family.

Reader Let us pray for a spirit of justice in the world, so that people of all races can come freely to God and grow closer to each other.
Lord, in your mercy. **Hear our prayer.**

Let us pray for God's blessing on all handicapped people. May blind and deaf people, those who are paralysed or cannot walk, be able to live a full and useful life.
Lord, in your mercy. **Hear our prayer.**

For the needs of Church leaders; that they will imitate Christ in their service of others

For parents and those who are preparing for marriage

For young people; that they will forgive the mistakes of their elders

Mary heard the words from the cross: 'Woman, behold your Son'. As her family, we ask her to pray with us as we say: **Hail Mary...**

We need silence to pray in our own way to the Father.

Celebrant Father, send your spirit of sonship on your people. Renew the commitment of their baptism, that they may heal those who have fallen into the power of evil. We make our prayer through Christ our Lord.

2nd SUNDAY IN ORDINARY TIME

Celebrant We remember today God's call to Israel and to ourselves, his new people. Let us respond to that call by praying for the Church and all mankind.

Reader We pray that all those who have been called and chosen to serve God, his Church and mankind in some special way may answer that call readily and willingly.
In your mercy, Lord. **Hear our prayer.**

We pray that all those chosen to be a light to the nations through their preaching and charity may continue in the strength to do God's will.
In your mercy, Lord. **Hear our prayer.**

For those in authority to know how to give way to others, if this is required by God's work

For the Jewish people, that they may obey God's call in whatever way it comes to them

For all who in their lifetime answer God's call, even unknowingly

Let us ask Mary, who responded so willingly to God's call, to pray with us that our response may be the same as hers. **Hail Mary...**

Let us ask God in silence that we may recognise his call, however it comes to us.

Celebrant Loving Father, you have called your people to know you and to follow your Son. Give them confidence in your love and help, so that they may never find your service a burden too heavy to bear. We ask this through Christ our Lord.

3rd SUNDAY IN ORDINARY TIME

Celebrant As members of the community of Christ, gathered to hear his word in the Gospel and to share the Bread of Life, let us pray for the Church and all mankind.

Reader We pray that all Christians may see Jesus as the light which shows the way to the Father. May their hearts be ready to receive his message and to carry it throughout the troubled world.
Let us pray. **Lord, may your kingdom come.**

We pray for blind people, that they may be able to lead a full life in communion and friendship with others, and feel the joy of the presence of Christ in their lives.
Let us pray. **Lord, may your kingdom come.**

For those whose life is cramped and joyless because of bad housing

For the people in underdeveloped countries, that their needs may not go unfilled through the plenty of others

For the victims of the recent disaster in...

Let us ask Mary our mother, who pondered God's word in her heart, to pray for us. **Hail Mary...**

In silence, let us put our prayers before Jesus who is our light.

Celebrant Father, help your Church to spread the kingdom of Christ by care and concern for all those in need and may our prayer reach out to all your children. Through Christ our Lord.

4th SUNDAY IN ORDINARY TIME

Celebrant Blessed are the poor in spirit, for the kingdom of heaven is theirs. Let us pray for this spirit to spread through the Church and to all mankind, so that all may come to share in the kingdom.

Reader We pray that all Christians may become more like Christ, in humility, generosity and wisdom, so that they may be able to show the world what the good news of his freedom really means.
Lord, in your mercy. **Hear our prayer.**

We pray that those who suffer may become more like Christ in their sufferings and that the world may come to see Christ suffering in them.
Lord, in your mercy. **Hear our prayer.**

For justice and peace for the Third World

For those who are crippled by poverty

For those adults who have recently chosen to follow Christ, that they may find support in his Church

The name of Mary is blessed by all nations, because of her poverty and faithfulness. We too call her blessed, and ask her to pray with us. **Hail Mary...**

Let us pray in silence.

Celebrant Lord God our Father, you gave your Son to the world to be a light to all nations. Open the eyes of your people to see his light, their ears to listen to his word, their mouths to proclaim his message. We ask this through the same Christ our Lord.

5th SUNDAY IN ORDINARY TIME

Celebrant Jesus came to bring light into the world. Through our prayers today, may this light touch the hearts of all men.

Reader Let us pray for all those who lack food to eat, clothes to wear, homes to keep them warm and protect them, that through the work of Christians and others they may come to have them.
Lord, hear us. **Lord, graciously hear us.**

Let us pray for the faith of Christian men and women to remain strong, whatever the doubts and uncertainties that beset them, so that they may overcome the disbelief and ignorance of the world.
Lord, hear us. **Lord, graciously hear us.**

For those who are blind, either because they cannot see or because they will not

For people who can find no purpose in life

For those who are searching for a meaning to their lives

We pray to Mary, the mother of Jesus, for her protection and guidance as we say. **Hail Mary...**

And now in the silence of our hearts we ask for that light which only our Lord can bring.

Celebrant Heavenly Father, remove from the hearts of your people unworthy affections, so that they may see your Son Jesus in those whom they seek to serve. We make this prayer through Christ our Lord.

6th SUNDAY IN ORDINARY TIME

Celebrant Let us pray to Christ who saw that love of God was the perfect fulfilment of the Law, and ask him to give his people that same wisdom.

Reader Christ fulfilled the Law and the prophets. May all Christians learn to be as singleminded and true as he was, in their dealings with God and men.

Lord, in your mercy. **Hear our prayer.**

Christ's word was always true and to be trusted. We pray that rulers and politicians may be honest in what they say and do.

Lord, in your mercy. **Hear our prayer.**

For business people, whether chairmen of multi-nationals or small shopkeepers, that they may deal in justice

For children, that they may find happiness in doing what is right

For lawyers and judges that they may always seek true and just judgement

Let us ask Mary to show us the wonder of God's Law and the joy of serving him. **Hail Mary...**

Let us listen in silence to God's Spirit within us.

Celebrant Lord of wisdom and truth, make your people ready at all times to study your law of love, and to serve you with joy. Through Christ our Lord.

7th SUNDAY IN ORDINARY TIME

Celebrant Let us pray to the God and Father of us all, whose Son commanded us to love even our enemies. In our prayers let us show that we are truly concerned for the welfare of others.

Reader As all receive unconditional love from God, we pray that they may give the same sort of love to their fellows, especially to those who do not show love to them.
In your mercy, Lord. **Hear our prayer.**

So that a spirit of truth may prevail in the world, we pray that all Christians may have the strength to proclaim the truth that brings peace.
In your mercy, Lord. **Hear our prayer.**

For those who work in public welfare, that they may act with humanity as well as justice

For architects, designers and builders, that they may see their work as a service for others

For those who wander from place to place, that they may find friendship

Now let us pray with Mary for all our friends and enemies.
Hail Mary...

Now let us pray in silence for all those in need.

Celebrant Heavenly Father, we leave our prayers in your hands, confident that you will grant whatever is for our lasting good. We make our prayer through Christ our Lord.

8th SUNDAY IN ORDINARY TIME

Celebrant God never forgets us. Our lives are always in his sight. Let us now lay our prayers before him, for the needs of the world.

Reader We pray that the world may get its priorities right; that its rulers may concentrate on what really matters and not advance their own interests at the expense of others.
Lord, hear us. **Lord, hear us always.**

We pray for those who are judged harshly by others; that they may not become bitter but may trust in God's mercy and justice.
Lord, hear us. **Lord, hear us always.**

For those who suffer from anxiety and nerves

For those who are short of the bare necessities of life

For those who bear heavy responsibilities

Mary placed her whole life trustfully in God's hands. Let us ask for her help. **Hail Mary...**

Let us pray silently for a moment.

Celebrant Father of all things, take these needs into your loving care. Answer our prayers in the name of Jesus your Son.

9th SUNDAY IN ORDINARY TIME

Celebrant Let us now make known to God our Father our prayers for the Church and the world.

Reader We pray that all Christians may possess the great gift of discernment, so that when they have to make choices, they will choose what is best.
Lord, hear us. **Lord, graciously hear us.**

We pray that those who lead in the Church and those who are led may all build their lives firmly on God's word, and be ready to listen to it in others.
Lord, hear us. **Lord, graciously hear us.**

For those in responsible positions who have to make hard decisions

For those recently retired and finding it hard to readjust

For doctors and nurses

We now ask our Lady to share her prayers with us.
Hail Mary...

Let us now pray in silence for all those in need.

Celebrant Father, listen to our prayers which we confidently make to you, through Jesus Christ our Lord.

10th SUNDAY IN ORDINARY TIME

Celebrant Abraham's faith was complete and unwavering. In the understanding of his belief let us pray:

Reader That the faith of God's people does not remain empty words, but that it be fired with faithful love and living belief, we pray to the Lord.
We ask this with faith. **Lord hear our prayer.**

That the Church's love of Christ may be made visible in its actions on behalf of the poor of the world, we pray to the Lord.
We ask this with faith. **Lord hear our prayer.**

For those whose faith is being tried by persecution

For the hungry of the world

For the sick and the old

With Mary, the Mother of God, we pray that we may hold fast to our faith in her Son. **Hail Mary...**

Let us pray in silence for God's will to be done.

Celebrant Father, we know that without the gift of your Spirit we cannot call Jesus Saviour, or call you Father. Help our unbelief and our lack of hope, so that we may preserve steadfastly in our belief, love and service of you and of our fellow-men through Christ our Lord.

11th SUNDAY IN ORDINARY TIME

Celebrant Jesus taught us by word and example that we should pray to the Father. So let us now pray to him with one heart and voice, for the Church and for all mankind.

Reader Let us pray that the Lord will send labourers into the harvest of souls. May more young men and women respond to his call to the priesthood and the religious life.
Lord, in your mercy. **Hear our prayer.**

Let us pray that lay people will continue to sacrifice their time selflessly in the service of others.
Lord, in your mercy. **Hear our prayer.**

For sinners, that they may be reconciled and understand that Jesus died for them

For the bishops, successors to the apostles, that they may be true shepherds to their flocks

For the sick and the dying, that they may find comfort.

Let us pray with Mary, the Mother of God and our mother also. **Hail Mary...**

In silence let us consider God's gifts to us.

Celebrant God our Father, your people come to you in humble prayer confident in your unfailing love. Hear the prayers we make today and grant them in accordance with your will, through Christ our Lord.

12th SUNDAY IN ORDINARY TIME

Celebrant Let us pray to God from whom comes everything that is good, and say, Lord, hear our prayer.

Reader Let us pray that Christians may have the courage and conviction to proclaim the Gospel bodly, openly and uncompromisingly to all people, so that they can come closer to Christ.
Lord, hear our prayer. **Lord, hear our prayer.**

Let us pray that the Church may work to bring the light of God's salvation to all people, carrying the torch of Christ's witness, and kindled with the fire of the Holy Spirit.
Lord, hear our prayer. **Lord, hear our prayer.**

That young people through their enthusiasm may work for peace

That Christians may recognise the presence of God in all people today

That all people be loving and caring with those who are close to them

Let us ask our Lady who stood beside the cross when others had run away to pray with us. **Hail Mary...**

Let us pray in silence to God our Father.

Celebrant Lord God our Father, you give all good things. Give your people confidence to proclaim your loving word to all mankind. We ask this through your Son, our Lord, Jesus Christ.

13th SUNDAY IN ORDINARY TIME

Celebrant Because we have been baptised and share in Christ's own life, we can pray to the Father in his name.

Reader Let us pray for the Church in every continent, that it may prefer nothing to Christ, and gladly divest itself of anything that obscures his living word.
Lord, hear us. **Lord, graciously hear us.**

Let us pray that God's people everywhere may begin this week with their faith strengthened, their hope increased, and their willingness to serve in love renewed.
Lord, hear us. **Lord, graciously hear us.**

For those brought low by temptation, depression or worry

For those whose hearts have been broken, and for those whose friends have left them

For those who brighten men's lives by drama and art, by music and song, by comedy and sport

Let us ask Mary, who pondered God's message in her heart, to help us keep God's words to us in our hearts.
Hail Mary...

In a few moments of silence we speak to God in our own words.

Celebrant Lord God our Father, you have brought salvation to the world through your Son Jesus Christ. May all who have been baptised in your name remain faithful to his word through the working of the Holy Spirit.

14th SUNDAY IN ORDINARY TIME

Celebrant The Father makes known the secrets of his kingdom to those who are gentle and lowly in heart. Let us pray that all God's people may welcome with humility the good news of the kingdom.

Reader We pray that God's people may learn to seek the kingdom proclaimed by God's Son as one of gentleness and humility, justice, love and peace, May they learn to make that kingdom come.

Lord, may your kingdom come. **And your will be done on earth.**

We pray that the Church may learn to read the signs of the times and work for a more just and peaceful world, with the faith and perseverance to carry on this work from day to day.

Lord, may your kingdom come. **And your will be done on earth.**

For those who bear a heavy burden of sickness, failure or anxiety, that they may accept Christ's gentle invitation to find rest in him

For those who have died, that they may find rest

For those who bear a heavy burden, that they may find ways of sharing it

May Mary, the lowly handmaid of the Lord, join her prayer to ours. **Hail Mary...**

Now in trustful, silent prayer, let us be with our Lord.

Celebrant Father, your Son rejoiced because you reveal the deepest secrets of your kingdom to your children. Keep alive in us this gift of faith, that we may never fail to trust in you. We make our prayer through Christ our Lord.

15th SUNDAY IN ORDINARY TIME

Celebrant The Gospel today gives us every reason to be confident. So let us ask God our Father to satisfy the needs of men everywhere.

Reader Let us ask God to inspire young people to offer themselves as labourers for God's kingdom.
Lord, save your people. **Lord, save your people.**

Let us pray that our own parish may be a living example of Christ's loving care in our world.
Lord, save your people. **Lord, save your people.**

For those who are working to make the world's food supply more plentiful

For all people in the world who do not have enough to eat

For those people whose conditions of life make it hard for them to see that God is good and to believe in him

Let us ask Mary, our mother, to add her prayers to ours. **Hail Mary...**

Let us pray in silence for our own intentions.

Celebrant Father, you have called your people to follow you. Give them the strength to go on doing so, come what may. We make our prayer through Christ our Lord.

16th SUNDAY IN ORDINARY TIME

Celebrant All the nations shall come to adore the Lord and glorify his name, for he does marvellous things and holy is his name. Let us come to the Lord and pray with faith for all mankind.

Reader We pray for a spirit of understanding so that Christians may grasp the message of the parables and grow in faith.
Lord, hear us. **Lord, graciously hear us.**

We pray for God's Church, that it may be a sign to the world of peace, brotherhood and charity.
Lord, hear us. **Lord, graciously hear us.**

For the Church wherever it is silenced and oppressed by military or totalitarian regimes

For all those who may have been hurt through our faults

For people displaced from their homes, for all who seek new roots, especially among us

Mary stored up many things in her heart and pondered on them. Let us pray with her for a deeper understanding. **Hail Mary...**

In the silence of our hearts let us pray for those intentions that we cannot put into words.

Celebrant Father, it is your Spirit who prays on our behalf and so it is with confidence that we make these prayers through Christ our Lord.

17th SUNDAY IN ORDINARY TIME

Celebrant God's ways are not our ways, and our ways are not his. As we come together to pray for the needs of his people, let us try to ask only for what gives glory to him and is of real value to his people.

Reader That we may be open to the promptings of the Spirit, leading us to recognise his will in the daily events and ordinary circumstances of our lives.
Lord, in your mercy. **Hear our prayer.**

That those in positions of power and government may be wise enough to place the needs of their fellow citizens before self interest.
Lord, in your mercy. **Hear our prayer.**

That parents and teachers may set a good example to their children

That those in authority may come to understand that the fear of the Lord is the beginning of wisdom

That those people who are not clever as the world understands may be seen to share in God's wisdom

Calling to mind the wisdom of the blessed Virgin, let us now pray with her. **Hail Mary...**

In a moment of silence let us wait upon the Lord.

Celebrant God our Father, your gift of wisdom comes through your Holy Spirit. Give us the humility to learn from the lesson of daily life what you would have us do in your service, through Christ our Lord.

18th SUNDAY IN ORDINARY TIME

Celebrant As all who come to Jesus in the right spirit were rewarded, so let us pray that all today may seek and find the love that really satisfies.

Reader We pray for justice and mercy to be shown to those who are starved of food and of friendship. May Christians be generous with the gift not only of their belongings, but also of themselves.

Lord of justice and mercy. **May your kingdom come.**

We pray for those who lose heart. May they learn that the love of Jesus is a pearl of great price, and that nothing and no one can separate them from his love

Lord of justice and mercy. **May your kingdom come.**

We pray for those who are unable to make a commitment to life and love

For those who have had to pay for love and friendship

For those who are rich but who have few friends

Mary shared the little she had with the Holy Spirit. The fruit of her emptiness became the Bread of Life. May she teach us to share ourselves with the world. **Hail Mary...**

All growth is quiet. We pause to say Amen to the Holy Spirit.

Celebrant Father, your Son was open to those in need. Help us to be careless in giving. We make our prayer in his name, Jesus the Lord.

19th SUNDAY IN ORDINARY TIME

Celebrant Elijah found God in the gentle breeze. The apostles found peace in the presence of Jesus. Let us ask God that all may recognise his presence in their lives.

Reader Let us pray that all God's people may learn to see his actions at work in the little and ordinary, and learn from them.
In your mercy, Lord. **Hear our prayer.**

May Christians recognise the gift of peace, and in their contacts with people try to be peacemakers.
In your mercy, Lord. **Hear our prayer.**

For a spirit of peace in the Church

For a peaceful solution where there is war or terrorism

For an end to all bitterness based on religious creeds

Let us ask Mary, herself a Jew, to pray with us for the Jewish People. **Hail Mary...**

In silence and peace let us listen to the voice of the Lord.

Celebrant God our loving Father, hear our prayers, and in the storms of life give your people courage and peace. We ask this through your Son, who walked on the waters of chaos and brought life out of death, Jesus Christ our Lord.

20th SUNDAY IN ORDINARY TIME

Celebrant God offers salvation, not only to those who call themselves Christians, but to all men who genuinely seek him. Let us pray for all who are looking for God.

Reader Remembering the love and mercy God shows to all, of whatever faith, we pray that those who seek may find what they are looking for.
Lord, in your mercy. **Hear our prayer.**

That Christians may not put obstacles in the way of others by their non-Christian behaviour, we pray to the Lord.
Lord, in your mercy. **Hear our prayer.**

That we may be freed from prejudice

That all Christians may be united in faith

That all refugees, in mind or body, may find a home

All of us, Christians and non-Christians, are sinners. Let us ask Mary to pray for us. **Hail Mary...**

In silence let us put our own needs as Christians before God.

Celebrant Father, we pray for the whole world which your Son redeemed, the world for which he died. May he draw all men to you, through the power of the Spirit.

21st SUNDAY IN ORDINARY TIME

Celebrant With Peter we acknowledge Jesus as the Christ, the Son of the living God, Let us pray in confidence to the Father in his name.

Reader That the world may take up the challenge of Jesus, and all those who seek the truth about him come to know who he is, we pray to the Lord.
Lord, hear us. **Lord graciously hear us.**

That the Church, built on the foundation of Peter and the apostles, may ever continue to renew itself so that it may be a source of inspiration and confidence to all Christian people, we pray to the Lord.
Lord, hear us. **Lord graciously hear us.**

That those who exercise authority may do so justly

That those members of the Church who dislike change may find trust and peace

That those who cling to past authority may come to see Christ in the Church today

May Mary, the Mother of the Church, pray for us. **Hail Mary...**

Let us open to the Father the secrets of our hearts, what we most deeply desire for ourselves and those we love.

Celebrant Father, you have called your people to be your Church, the community of faith. May we faithfully share in the task of working for the coming of your Kingdom. We make this prayer through Christ the Lord.

22nd SUNDAY IN ORDINARY TIME

Celebrant God is merciful and always ready to help us start again. Let us pray for all who seek to follow his will

Reader We pray that a spirit of confidence in God's will may prevail in the Church, that it may think in God's way and not fall victim to illusions and distractions.
Lord, hear us. **Lord graciously hear us.**

We pray for all those who are imprisoned and tortured for following the dictates of their conscience, that they may be strengthened and comforted.
Lord, hear us. **Lord graciously hear us.**

For justice in the European Community

For students in local schools and colleges

For those who are bringing in the harvest

Mary was redeemed and glorified through suffering. Let us ask her prayers in our need. **Hail Mary...**

Let us now pray in silence

Celebrant Heavenly Father, we make our prayers through your Son who rose from the dead for our salvation. Accept our worship in spirit and in truth and grant us a share in his glory, who lives and reigns for ever.

23rd SUNDAY IN ORDINARY TIME

Celebrant Jesus assures us that when two or three ask anything in his name it will be granted by our Father in heaven. It is with this confidence that we now pray together.

Reader We pray that all people may come to see themselves as members of one family, sharing the strengths and weaknesses of a community. May they be constructive in criticism and gentle in judgement of one another.
Lord, hear us. **Lord graciously hear us.**

We pray that the sacrament of Reconciliation may be an opportunity for people to make a new start so that they look to the future rather than dwell on the failures of the past.
Lord, hear us. **Lord graciously hear us.**

For those who are married, that they may recognise that love flourishes on praise and forgiveness

For those in prison, that they may use their time as an opportunity for growth and change

For those in authority, that they may exercise power with gentleness, recognising the freedom of the individual

The love of a mother for her children remains true whatever may happen. In confidence we turn to Mary and pray. **Hail Mary...**

Let us pray for a moment in silence

Celebrant Heavenly Father, your weak people find it hard to remain true to their vocation as followers of Jesus. Send your Spirit into their hearts so that they may remain faithful to the command of love your Son gave them. We make our prayer in his name, Jesus the Lord.

24th SUNDAY IN ORDINARY TIME

Celebrant Remembering that God constantly forgives all faults, let us pray to him for a like spirit of forgiveness in the world.

Reader Let us ask our Lord to remove all feelings of resentment and revenge from his people, and to replace them with a spirit of mutual forgivnesss.
Lord, have mercy. **Lord, have mercy.**

Let us ask him who heals all ills and removes all guilt to make his people grateful for his love and compassion.
Lord, have mercy. **Lord, have mercy.**

On those who prolong feuds between countries

On those involved in family quarrels

On those whose temperament makes it hard for them to forgive

Let us commend ourselves to Mary, so deeply wounded by the death of her Son. **Hail Mary...**

In silence let us try to appreciate the forgiveness of God.

Celebrant God our Father, you freely and generously forgive your people's sins. Accept our sorrow for our hard and unforgiving spirit, and lead us to a richer life through Christ our Lord.

25th SUNDAY IN ORDINARY TIME

Celebrant We are encouraged to develop our attitudes towards work. Let us pray to our Father for the working needs of mankind.

Reader Let us pray that all men and women may learn to work conscientiously for one another, and so experience the joy that comes from work well done.
We ask this with faith. **Lord, hear our prayer.**

Let us pray for those who are out of work at this time, and ask that they may find real and practical help.
We ask this with faith. **Lord, hear our prayer.**

For a fuller life for the sick and the handicapped who are unable to earn their own living

For those who have work, that they may grow through their labour

For the establishment and maintenance of good industrial relations at work

Let us join in prayer with Mary, our mother. **Hail Mary...**

Let us pause to pray for those we work with.

Celebrant Heavenly Father, we offer you our labours; we ask you to bless them and to help us always to give of our best, through Christ our Lord.

26th SUNDAY IN ORDINARY TIME

Celebrant God's ways are just, but we do not mirror his justice. Let us place the world's problems in his hands.

Reader Let us pray for our society and especially for young people; that they may learn to base their lives not on competition but on sympathy with the interests of others.
Lord of love and justice. **May your kingdom come.**

Let us pray for all Christian people; may they show their faith in generous action on behalf of others, not in an outward show of piety.
Lord of love and justice. **May your kingdom come.**

For economic justice in the world

For a moral renewal of society

For the unity of the Church

Let us call on Mary to pray with us. **Hail Mary...**

Let us pray for a moment for our personal intentions.

Celebrant Father, you want your people to live in peace and justice. help us to grow in unity of heart and mind, as we respond to your call, through Jesus Christ our Lord.

27th SUNDAY IN ORDINARY TIME

Celebrant Let us pray to God who has dominion over everything he creates and to whom all will one day return.

Reader Let us pray that whatever situations people find themselves in, whether of success or failure, joy or sorrow, they will always trust the God we call Father, and place themselves in his hands.
Lord, hear us. **Lord graciously hear us.**

Let us pray that the Church may have the openness of heart, mind and spirit to recognise God's prophets today and to accept their message.
Lord, hear us. **Lord graciously hear us.**

For those who have just begun at school, college or work

For those who are sorrowing over a recent death

For those who have to work unsocial hours

Mary knew that her Son was the keystone of the building. Let us pray with her. **Hail Mary...**

In silence let us pray for what is close to our hearts

Celebrant Father, your people are those who seek to extend your kingdom. May we enlist ourselves among those who strive to make your kingdom come. We make our prayer through Christ our Lord.

28th SUNDAY IN ORDINARY TIME

Celebrant St Paul reminds us that there is nothing we cannot do if we have the help of the One who gives us strength. So with great confidence let us turn to the Father and ask him to show his will.

Reader We pray for those who refuse the Lord's invitation, that they may be helped to discover what they are being asked to do and who is asking them to do it.
In your mercy, Lord. **Hear our prayer.**

We pray for those who are troubled by difficulties, oppressed by suffering, who have lost trust, who have given way to despair, that they may discover the strength of their Saviour.
In your mercy, Lord. **Hear our prayer.**

For all road users, that they may always be mindful of their own safety and that of others

For all who receive God's call in any way, that they may answer it

For all who take God's gifts for granted, that they may be grateful

We now ask Mary to teach us to respond to God's invitation as willingly as she did. **Hail Mary...**

For a few moments let us now pray silently to God.

Celebrant Father, you love us for you have made us your children. Open our hearts to know and do your will, that we may live for ever and ever with you and Jesus Christ our Lord.

29th SUNDAY IN ORDINARY TIME

Celebrant God's people have to fight his battles. In doing this they must know that apart from the Lord they are nothing. Let us then pray:

Reader That his people will work for justice and the liberation of the oppressed, wherever and whenever oppression and domination are to be found, let us pray to the Lord.
Lord, hear our prayer. **And let our cry come to you.**

That his people will never assume that God is on their side, but always ask for his guidance in making judgements, remembering that all men are brothers, let us pray to the Lord.
Lord, hear your prayer. **And let our cry come to you.**

That God may bless other Churches, communities and their leaders, recalling that everyone has similar battles to fight

That God will guide us to befriend the lonely and share their problems

That God will cement family solidarity with loving-kindness and understanding between individual members

Let us pray that our Lady may help us never to falter, but always to have the courage to do the will of God.
Hail Mary...

Let us pray in silence for our own intentions.

Celebrant Lord, though our battles may be hard-won and we may have to fight them often, grant us the perservance to continue, and at the end of the day give us your peace, through Christ our Lord.

30th SUNDAY IN ORDINARY TIME

Celebrant God our Father brings us together so that we may praise and worship him, the creator and author of all good things. In our prayers, we show our faith in his providence, and our hope that his will may be accomplished.

Reader Let us pray for politicians and those in various positions of authority, that truth and justice may prevail in their decisions.
Lord, in your mercy. **Hear our prayer.**

Let us pray for justice to be shown to the poor, that the dealings of those in authority with them may be guided by a spirit of generosity rather than the letter of the law.
Lord, in your mercy. **Hear our prayer.**

For those who are searching for an experience of prayer

For those who are unable to worship with their fellow Christians today

For strangers and newcomers to this parish

Let us ask Mary, our mother, to pray with us.
Hail Mary...

Let us pray for a few moments in silence.

Celebrant Almighty Father, we make our prayer in faith, hoping that you will hear our petitions and enable us to serve you in love, through Christ our Lord.

31st SUNDAY IN ORDINARY TIME

Celebrant When we pray we acknowledge God's strength and men's weakness. So let us pray that his people will be infused with his strength.

Reader We pray to God that the faith of his people be not just a matter of words but of deeds performed in love.
Lord, show us your mercy and love. **And grant us your salvation.**

We pray for the government that it may be concerned for the good of all people, particularly the aged and the disabled.
Lord, show us your mercy and love. **And grant us your salvation.**

For missionaries in their work of spreading the Good News

For immigrants who are finding it difficult to settle down

For the schools of the district, the teachers, pupils and ancillary staff

Let us pray to Mary whose presence was a continual help to her Son in his ministry. **Hail Mary...**

Now in silence let us pray to the Lord.

Celebrant Almighty God, your Son suffered and died at the hands of men. Give us the courage to be living witnesses of our faith in good times and in bad. Bring us to the glory of the resurrection. We make this prayer through Christ our Lord.

32nd SUNDAY IN ORDINARY TIME

Celebrant Let us pray in confidence to God, whose care for his people is without limit, saying, Lord, show us your love.

Reader That the Father may give his people the wisdom to discover what is truly important, so that when the Lord comes they will recognise him and follow him,
Let us pray to the Lord. **Lord, show us your love.**

That those who rule us may be guided by the Father, and be inspired to give an example of justice, peace and truth,
Let us pray to the Lord. **Lord, show us your love.**

For the families of those who have died, that they may have faith and hope in the resurrection

For parents who want to bring their children up in the Church

For those who are scornful of the things of the Spirit

Let us pray to our Lady who always did the will of the Father. **Hail Mary...**

Let us now add silently our own intentions.

Celebrant Father, you give your people a sign of your loving care in the person of Jesus your Son. May he bring our prayers to you and grant us your peace. We ask this through the same Christ, your Son, our Lord.

33rd SUNDAY IN ORDINARY TIME

Celebrant Jesus the Lord has the message of eternal life. With this prayer in our hearts we make our petitions.

Reader That Christ, the good shepherd, will give guidance, courage and optimism to all those who hold office in the Church, we pray to the Lord.
Lord, hear us. **Lord graciously hear us.**

That Christ will give all members of his Church the good sense not to waste their talents, but to use them willingly and generously for the benefit of others, we pray to the Lord.
Lord, hear us. **Lord graciously hear us.**

For those who feel that they are foreigners among us

For those praying, hoping and waiting

For all who can help to break down barriers of race, creed or colour

We pray with Mary who bore for us the body of Christ. **Hail Mary...**

In a few moments of deep silence we allow God's spirit to pray within us.

Celebrant Lord God our Father, teach us your ways, lead us in your paths, through your son Jesus Christ.

34th SUNDAY IN ORDINARY TIME

Christ the King

Celebrant The Church of God lives always in the care of the Good Shepherd. Let us pray that it may remain ever responsive to his unfailing love.

Reader Let us pray that today's gospel may help Christians to look for their King among the poor, the hungry and the abandoned.
Guard us, good shepherd. **And lead us to the truth.**

Let us pray that the ever-watchful Shepherd of the flock may keep his sheep from straying, give them strength in their weakness, and light in their darkness.
Guard us, good shepherd. **And lead us to the truth.**

That Christians may always be generous in helping those in need

That all who do not hear and follow Christ may surrender gladly to his gentle kingship

That the Lord may give those who are facing death today the victory over this last enemy

Mary is the first of those who belong to Christ. By her prayer for us sinners may we too be made alive in him.
Hail Mary...

In silent prayer let us remember gratefully the tenderness and goodness of our God.

Celebrant Father, as a shepherd tends his flock so do you support and feed your people. We humbly ask the grace to be numbered among those at your Son's right hand when he comes again as King in glory. We make our prayer in his name, Jesus the Lord.

1st SUNDAY OF ADVENT

Celebrant During this season we are reminded that Jesus is always present. We pray that his people may be awake, sensitive and open to him.

Reader As we wait in joyful hope for the coming of our saviour, we pray that his birth may give birth to the brotherhod of all mankind.
Lord, be near us. **Lord, hear our prayer.**

Jesus was born in the darkness, that men might hope in the dawn. We pray that his hopeful people can bring good news to the sorrowful.
Lord, be near us. **Lord, hear our prayer.**

For those who have no knowledge of the joy God offers

For disarmament and the removal of the causes of violence

For scientists, thinkers and world leaders

May Mary, mother of Jesus and of all men, teach us to be sons of God and brothers and sisters to each other.
Hail Mary...

We remain quiet for a moment to allow God to rouse us from our sleep.

Celebrant Holy Spirit of love, renew the earth, bring men into communion and grant peace to all nations. We make our prayer through Christ our Lord.

2nd SUNDAY OF ADVENT

Celebrant Christians must turn away from all forms of prejudice and make peace with each other if they are to be true to their baptism. Let us pray for reconciliation, and for the coming of God's kingdom.

Reader We pray that the Church may be filled with the spirit of repentance and peace, helping to remove prejudice and calling all mankind to live in harmony and friendship.
Lord, hear our prayer. **And grant us your salvation.**

We pray that all bishops, priests and teachers be faithful to the true nature of God's kingdom. May they lead their people with sincerity and truthfulness.
Lord, hear our prayer. **And grant us your salvation.**

For unity among all Christians

For harmony among all members of the Church

For those who have recently died, and for their families

Let us ask Mary, the virgin mother of God, to pray for us. **Hail Mary...**

Let us pray quietly for a moment.

Celebrant Lord God, all reconciliation and peace comes from you. Grant that we may hear your Son and work eagerly for the coming of your kingdom. We make our prayer through Jesus Christ, our Lord.

3rd SUNDAY OF ADVENT

Celebrant The Church is awaiting the coming of the Son of God, who will save men from their sickness. Let us pray to him for healing, that the world may be saved.

Reader Let us pray that Christians may play a prophetic role in the world, helping the blind to see, the lame to walk, and all mankind to hear the Good News of Christ's coming.
Lord, hear our prayer. **And let our cry come to you.**

Let us pray for the Church waiting in patience for the coming of the Saviour: in its patience may it not forget to ask, and to receive in gratitude.
Lord, hear our prayer. **And let our cry come to you.**

For those cut off from others by age, sickness, or isolation

For those who will be celebrating Christmas without a loved husband, wife, parent or child

For those who are waiting anxiously for news from those they love

Mary waited for the birth of her Son with trust. Let us pray to her. **Hail Mary...**

In trustful silence let us pray for our personal intentions.

Celebrant Father, may your Spirit be with your Church so that it may continue the healing work of your Son, Jesus Christ the Lord.

4th SUNDAY OF ADVENT

Celebrant As we begin the last week of Advent let us make an effort to pause occasionally amid the bustle of last-minute preparations, and consider the Christian meaning of the feast of Christmas, as we pray for the needs of mankind.

Reader Let us pray that all God's beloved people may come to discover his grace and peace, and make them known to all mankind.

Lord, hear us. **Lord, graciously hear us.**

Let us pray that in the coming week Christians will try to share with others the joy and wonder that come with the birth of Emmanuel, 'God with us'.

Lord, hear us. **Lord, graciously hear us.**

For the homeless, remembering how the Holy Family had to search for a roof

For the old and sick, that they may have extra help and attention over the Christmas season

For all nations, that they may come to realise that Christmas is a time for peace

Let us pray that Mary, the mother of Jesus, will share her joy with us. **Hail Mary...**

Let us pray in silence for those we wish to pray for.

Celebrant Lord God our Father, may this time of preparation for the celebration of Christ's birthday remind your people that loving is giving. We make our prayer with Jesus our Saviour and Lord.

CHRISTMAS: MIDNIGHT MASS

Celebrant Unto us a child is born, unto us a son is given. As we celebrate the good news of our salvation let us approach the God and Father of our Lord Jesus Christ in confidence and love. We, too, are his sons and daughters, and he invites us to open our hearts and minds to him on behalf of mankind.

Reader Let us pray for all God's people as they celebrate together this holy feast in wonder: may they never grow tired of its message of hope and joy.
Lord, be with us. **Now and forever.**

Let us pray for all our fellow Christians, that filled with God's peace they may be moved to share that peace with others.
Lord, be with us. **Now and forever.**

Let us pray that the good news of Christ's coming may inspire the lives of all Christians, so that they may follow Christ in deed as well as word, showing him in the quality of their lives.
Lord, be with us. **Now and forever.**

Let us pray that as Christ became poor for our sake, so his Church may live in poverty of spirit, serving the poor of the world and in our society.
Lord, be with us. **Now and forever.**

With Mary the mother of our Lord let us rejoice together as we say. **Hail Mary...**

Let us be still for a moment to reflect on Christ's coming in the silence of the night and what it means for us.

Celebrant Pour forth, we beseech you O Lord, your grace into our hearts, that we to whom the Incarnation of Christ your Son was made known by the message of an angel, may by his passion and cross be brought to the glory of his resurrection, through the same Christ our Lord.

(Prayers for the Dawn Mass are on p. 118, and for the Midday Mass on p. 181.)

HOLY FAMILY

(1st Sunday after Christmas)

Celebrant We have been called together as parts of one Body; with this in mnd we make our prayer.

Reader For the whole family of the Church, that we may speak words of peace, perform deeds of love, and live in harmony with one another, we pray to the Lord.
Lord, hear us. **Lord graciously hear us.**

For those whose marriages have proved unhappy or impossible; for those who have had to go their separate ways; and for those who are trying to forgive and forget, we pray to the Lord.
Lord, hear us. **Lord graciously hear us.**

For parents disappointed by their children; for children unable to understand their parents; and for those in any kind of family upset or quarrel, we pray to the Lord.
Lord, hear us. **Lord graciously hear us.**

For unmarried mothers, and unmarried fathers; for children suffering because they are unloved or ignored; for families damaged by gossip or slander, we pray to the Lord.
Lord, hear us. **Lord graciously hear us.**

For our own families, that rising above differences of age and outlook, we may learn to love one another, we pray to the Lord.
Lord, hear us. **Lord graciously hear us.**

We seek the prayer of St Joseph and our Lady for the whole family of the living, the living dead, and the children yet unborn. **Hail Mary...**

In a few moments of silence let us ask God's blessing on parents, brothers and sisters, and our wider families.

Celebrant Lord God, keep us for ever united in love for you and for one another. Through Christ our Lord.

THE OCTAVE OF CHRISTMAS

The Solemnity of Mary, Mother of God

Celebrant As we praise God for his generous blessings, let us pray for all God's people at the start of a new year.

Reader We pray that as we have welcomed the Christ child this Christmas, so all those in need may find shelter and rest.
Lord, you are the hope of your people. **Hear our prayer**

We pray that the New Year may bring peace and good will among men of every creed, class and colour.
Lord, you are the hope of your people. **Hear our prayer.**

For those who are not free to worship God openly

For those who suffer because one they love has died

For peace and satisfaction in industry

Remembering Mary's role in the drama of salvation, let us join our prayers with hers as we say together. **Hail Mary...**

Let us pray for a moment in silence.

Celebrant Almighty God and Father, we are full of the joys of this season. Help us to share our happiness and our goods with others, as our gift to Christ the newborn King, who reigns for ever and ever.

2nd SUNDAY AFTER CHRISTMAS

Celebrant We can know God only through Jesus, who was born into our world and lived a human life. Let us pray that by the light of Jesus all mankind may grow in knowledge of God.

Reader Let us pray for the world, which God's Son came to live in and remain in for ever through the gift of his Spirit.
Lord, in your mercy. **Hear our prayer**

Let us pray for all Christians, that Christ may live in their hearts through their faith, and speak and act through them.
Lord, in your mercy. **Hear our prayer.**

For those who rule nations, that his Spirit may enter into their hearts

For the bishops, that they may work together

For all Christians, that they may witness to Jesus by their lives

Jesus is our light and life. Let us ask Mary, his mother, to present our prayers to her Son. **Hail Mary..**

Let us pray silently for what we desire.

Celebrant God our Father, unite all those who bear the name of Christian, that the world may believe in Jesus Christ whom you have sent.

THE EPIPHANY

Celebrant Today we celebrate the revelation of the Son of God to the whole world. Let us pray that people everywhere will come to recognise him.

Reader We pray for the poor and needy of the world, remembering that Christ showed himself to them and shows himself to us through them now.
We pray to you, Lord. **Lord. hear our prayer.**

We pray for missionaries, that they may find strength in the task of spreading knowledge of Christ to those who do not know how to recognize him.
We pray to you, Lord. **Lord, hear our prayer.**

For honesty and integrity amongst statesmen and diplomats

For justice and peace in industry

For sorrow for the compromise of Christian principles in private and in public life

Let us ask Mary, the mother of Jesus Christ, our Lord and Saviour, to pray for us. **Hail Mary...**

Let us pray in silence that Jesus may be revealed to us.

Celebrant Father, we ask you to continue to show us your Son, so that his work may fill the world, through the power of his Holy Spirit. We make our prayer in his name, Jesus the Lord.

ASH WEDNESDAY

Celebrant We are now entering a period of prayer and penance. Let us pray to God that it may serve to make the world return to him.

Reader We pray for tranquility in this busy world, so that people everywhere may have time to listen to God and discover his will.
Lord, hear us. **Lord, graciously hear us.**

We pray for a spirit of generosity in dealings between nations, so that those who have nothing may have the means of finding God.
Lord, hear us. **Lord, graciously hear us.**

We pray for a spirit of restraint in our society, so that what it can produce may be fairly shared.
Lord, hear us. **Lord, graciously hear us.**

For the Pope and the bishops, who are Christ's special ambassadors

For handicapped people, who are Christ's special friends

Let us share our time of prayer with Mary, the mother of our Saviour. **Hail Mary...**

We must spend time in the desert if we are to know God. Let us be with him now in silence.

Celebrant Father, your Son was led by the Spirit into the desert. We pray that we may be driven by the same Spirit to watch and pray, so that we may not enter into temptation. We make our prayer through Christ Jesus our Lord.

1st SUNDAY OF LENT

Celebrant It is God's will that all men should be saved through Christ our Lord. So let us pray for the salvation of the whole world.

Reader We pray for the Church throughout the world. May it have the courage that was Christ's in his temptations, and remain steadfast in its actions and teaching.
Lord, hear us. **Lord, graciously hear us.**

We pray for the Churches of our country. May they set aside all bitterness between them by the power of the Holy Spirit and live in harmony and peace.
Lord, hear us. **Lord, graciously hear us.**

For missionaries who are tempted to water down te Gospel

For artists and scholars whose vision may seem preferable to the Gospel

For political prisoners who may despair of the power of the Gospel

Let us ask our Lady for her help. **Hail Mary...**

We pray in silence for our own needs.

Celebrant Father, you sent your Son to save all men. May his obedience bring salvation to all for whom we pray. We make our prayer through Christ our Lord.

2nd SUNDAY OF LENT

Celebrant The Father calls us to listen to his Son. We can be sure that his Son will in turn listen to us, so with great trust let us ask in Jesus's name for all that we pray for.

Reader We pray for Christians throughout the world, that they may listen to the Lord's voice and be able to obey him without fear.
Lord, in your mercy. **Hear our prayer.**

We pray for the Christian communities of our country, that when they are gathered together in Christ's name they may be a sign of faith and love.
Lord, in your mercy. **Hear our prayer.**

For other Christians, that all may be one

For those who are sick, that they may be strengthened

For our absent friends, that they may be safe and happy

Mary knew her Son in all his moods, and lives with him now in his glory. Let us ask her to join with our prayers now and at the hour of our death. **Hail Mary...**

Let us pray for a moment quietly.

Celebrant Lord God our Father, you sent your Son to carry a message of salvation to the world. May your people continue his work through the power of the Spirit. We ask this through Jesus Christ your Son, our Lord.

3rd SUNDAY OF LENT

Celebrant Only Jesus can satisfy our thirst for happiness. So we turn to him in our prayer, and ask for the gift of his life for all mankind.

Reader We pray for those who are searching for a full life, that they may find the spring of living water that is Christ.
In your mercy, Lord. **Hear our prayer.**

We pray for the casualties of broken marriages, that they may find love and affection again and may not lose faith in God or in men.
In your mercy, Lord. **Hear our prayer.**

For those who work with addicts and alcoholics

For motorists, that they may realise their responsibilities

For all those deprived of their human rights

Let us pray with Mary that we may always be close to her Son. **Hail Mary...**

Conscious of our sinfulness we turn to Jesus, seeking in our silent prayer the life that only he can give.

Celebrant Lord Jesus, we know that you are the saviour of the world. Answer our prayers and give us a share in your life, for ever and ever.

4th SUNDAY OF LENT

Celebrant Lord of light and truth, look upon your people who stumble in darkness. Listen to the cry we lift to you from this valley of shadows.

Reader We pray that all God's people, who see the truth only dimly as in a dark mirror, may have their faith strengthened and see Christ as the light of the world.
Lord, be our light. **Lord, be our light.**

We pray that renewal in the Church may be a true renewal in the hearts of all its members, inspired by a hard look into the depths of their being during this Lent.
Lord, be our light. **Lord, be our light.**

For the blind

For those who find life meaningless

For Christian thinkers and writers

Mary walked always in the light. Let us pray with her.
Hail Mary...

Let us look beyond the mirror into our true selves and pray for a moment about what we find there.

Celebrant Father, you have brought us out of darkness into the truth. Grant to us all the grace to live in your light, and to stay clear of illusions and self deception. We ask this through Jesus Christ, who is the light of the world.

5th SUNDAY OF LENT

Celebrant The death of Lent is only a preparation for the new life of Easter. Therefore we pray that the world may die to sin and live a new life in Christ.

Reader That Christians everywhere may seek out those habits of sin which mean death to the soul, and so come with joy to the celebration of Easter, we pray to the Lord.
Lord, in your mercy. **Hear our prayer.**

That the people of God may believe ever more firmly in the resurrection of the body, we pray to the Lord.
Lord, in your mercy. **Hear our prayer.**

For the dying, that they may look forward to their resurrection

For the custodians of the law, that they may rule with justice and mercy

For our priests, that they might have courage and perseverance

Let us pray that Mary may be our constant companion in times of both joy and sorrow. **Hail Mary...**

Let us pray in peaceful silence.

Celebrant Heavenly Father, your Son came to bring life to a world dead in sin. Give your people a spirit of repentance that they may rise to a new life in Christ, who lives and reigns for ever.

6th SUNDAY OF LENT

Passion Sunday

Celebrant Jesus shows us the way to life. It is the path of loving obedience to the Father. It costs no less than everything and so we ask that his people remain faithful to his way.

Reader We pray for the Pilgrim Church on earth. May its members have the courage to take up their cross and follow him who will lead it to share in his resurrection.
We pray to the Lord. **Lord, keep us true to your way.**

We pray for all those who are crucified with Christ through oppression and torture. May the world see in them the face of Christ, whose cross and resurrection set us free.
We pray to the Lord. **Lord, keep us true to your way.**

For all who have not learned to empty themselves of sin

For those who, weighed down with hardship, failure or distress, feel that God is far from them

For those who suffer through temptation

Before all others in the Church, Mary follows in the footsteps of her Son. Her prayer for us sustains us on our journey. **Hail Mary...**

In our silent prayer may a loving God reveal his closeness to us.

Celebrant Father, in a fallen world your Son was perfectly obedient to your will. May his obedience even unto death be for your people now the way to our true life. We make our prayer in his name, Jesus Christ our Lord.

MAUNDY THURSDAY

Our Lord and Master became the sacrificial Lamb, who lived and died for others. Let us pray that men will live and die following this example. So with him we pray: Father, your will be done.

We pray for the whole Church, the living body of Christ. May the members of this Body always be willing to give themselves generously for the world.
We pray with Christ. **Father, your will be done.**

We pray for the Jewish people, against whom Christians have sinned. May they come to a fulfilment of their hopes through Jesus, the Saviour of the world.
We pray with Christ. **Father, your will be done.**

For those in the agony of a breakdown, that they may find support and encouragement

For the gift of humility, and for those who have found the lowest place

For priests, that they may offer Mass with conviction, and live it in their lives

Tonight, recalling Mary's pain as she prayed for her Son at the hour of his death we ask her to pray for us.
Hail Mary...

Let us pray in silence that we may not be put to the test.

Celebrant Father, you have given us in Jesus an example of perfect love. Teach us this sacrificial love so that nothing will separate us from him who lives with you now and always.

EASTER SUNDAY

Celebrant Let us pray to God, the almighty Father, who raised his Son Jesus from the dead. Let us ask him that all his people may share in the glory of the resurrection.

Reader Let us pray for Christians throughout the world. May they remain true to the new life they received at baptism and live always with the life of the risen Christ.
Lord, in your mercy. **Hear our prayer.**

Let us pray for all those who this Easter have received new life by baptism. May they discover the face of the risen Christ in their new brothers and sisters in the Lord.
Lord, in your mercy. **Hear our prayer.**

For the spread of the Gospel among those who know nothing of the resurrection

For the sick and dying whom Christ invites in a special way to share in his sufferings so as to share in his resurrection

For the Church, that its faith in the resurrection may be strengthened

Let us pray to Mary, who was filled with joy at her Son's being raised from the dead. **Hail Mary...**

Let us contemplate the risen Christ in silence.

Celebrant Father, it is because of your Son's death and resurrection, and the power of the Holy Spirit, that our prayers are surely heard by you. Guide us today that we may be found worthy to share the resurrection of your Son, who lives and reigns for ever.

2nd SUNDAY OF EASTER

Celebrant St Peter has reminded us of the joy we should have because we are Christians, and because we know Christ is risen. Let us now turn to God in prayer.

Reader We pray that the Church will remain always faithful to the teaching of the apostles, especially as handed down in the tradition of the breaking of bread.
Listen to us, Lord. **And hear our prayer.**

We pray that God's people will recognise and accept God's call in their daily lives, and carry out the mission they are called to perform.
Listen, to us Lord. **And hear our prayer.**

For those who have found no purpose in life and who wander from place to place

For the false prophets who try to lead others astray

For those on holiday

We share our faith in the risen Christ with Mary, his mother, and with all the saints. **Hail Mary...**

Let us now express our thoughts and prayers silently.

Celebrant God our Father, you have given your people new birth as your sons and daughters, so that they might have a sure and firm hope. We pray that we may always enjoy this hope through Christ our Lord.

3rd SUNDAY OF EASTER

Celebrant God reveals himself in Christ, the Word made flesh. We are in touch with him when we listen to the scriptures and share in the breaking of the bread. United with him here and now, let us pray to the Father.

Reader Let us pray that the Church remain faithful to its trust in the risen Lord, and like the first generation of Christians continue to share his gifts with others.
We pray to the Lord. **Lord, hear our prayer.**

We pray for those who perpetuate violence, that they may be confounded, confused and converted by the love and forgiveness of their victims.
We pray to the Lord. **Lord, hear our prayer.**

For a continued sense of wonder as we celebrate Mass together

For a knowledge and understanding of scripture

For those who look after the sick

Sharing our Lady's Easter joy, let us pray. **Hail Mary...**

In silence let us allow our hearts to burn within us as we stand before the Father.

Celebrant Father, increase your Easter joy within us by helping us discover the limitless richness of the scriptures. Nourish our minds with what we hear and read, and strengthen us through the healing of the bread of eternal life, through Christ our Lord.

4th SUNDAY OF EASTER

Celebrant Today's gospel shows us Jesus as our shepherd. Let us ask the help of our Lord for all who lead, protect or guide others.

Reader For our chief bishop the Pope, and for all the bishops, who have been given the responsibility of being shepherds. May they lead their people, but allow all their rightful freedom.
Let us pray to the Lord. **Christ our Shepherd, hear us.**

For parents and teachers, that they may remember that they lead others to God by the example of their lives more than by what they say.
Let us pray to the Lord. **Christ our Shepherd, hear us.**

For missionaries, and all who serve God in places where responsibility may entail danger

For people who have strayed from the Church, that they may find a welcome when they return

For the dying, that they may experience the love and care of the Good Shepherd

Let us ask Mary, who had the responsibility and joy of bringing up God's Son, to pray with us for all who depend on us. **Hail Mary...**

Let us in silence ask God to give us the qualities of the shepherd: care, concern, courage and love.

Celebrant God our Father, who raised from the dead our Lord Jesus Christ, the great Shepherd of his people, hear our prayers, and give to all who have responsibility for others a share in his loving Spirit. We ask this for his sake.

5th SUNDAY OF EASTER

Celebrant The unity of Jesus and his Father is a great source of joy for the Christian. We commit ourselves to Jesus by our baptism, seeking eternal life with the Father. So with joyful confidence we make our prayer together today.

Reader We pray for the members of the Church, that like the early Christians, they may fulfil their vocation through sharing bread and spreading the word of God.
Listen to us, Lord. **And hear our prayer.**

We pray for those young men and women who offer themselves to the service of God in the ministry. May their generosity be rewarded by a fruitful harvest as they seek to bring many to knowledge and love of God and their fellows.
Listen, to us Lord. **And hear our prayer.**

For deacons, both those preparing for the priesthood, and those combining their service with the vocation of marriage

For those organisations which prevent cruelty to animals and so protect the dignity of man

For our police men and women, that they may serve us with patience and justice

We pray with great confidence that Mary's prayers will not fail us, as we say. **Hail Mary...**

With joy in the presence of the risen Christ among us we pray silently for our needs.

Celebrant Heavenly Father, hear our prayers, those spoken and those which remain in our hearts. Grant what we ask through the power of the risen Christ who lives and reigns with you for ever.

6th SUNDAY OF EASTER

Celebrant Lord God, through Jesus you show us the mystery of your love. Through him you send your Spirit into the world. Do not now turn away from the prayers we offer you.

Reader Let us pray for those who have faith, that they may be able to share it with others with courtesy and the strength that comes from a life that reflects their hope.
Loving Lord, hear us. **Lord hear us.**

Let us pray for those who have no faith, that they may not be left orphans, but may receive the Spirit of truth.
Loving Lord, hear us. **Lord hear us.**

For those who are lonely

For missionaries who proclaim the Christ

For the forgotten dead

Let us ask for the help of our Blessed Lady. **Hail Mary...**

Let us pray about the problems close to our hearts.

Celebrant Lord of love and hopefulness, hear the prayers which we offer in the name of Jesus, and answer them through his grace.

ASCENSION DAY

Celebrant God sent his Son to save mankind, so let us pray to him in confidence for the needs of all his people.

Reader Let us pray for the Church, that it may respond to Christ's call and reveal to all the presence of him who reigns in heaven but continues to live among us.
Lord, we pray. **Lord, hear our prayer.**

Let us pray that all Christians may learn to live according to the commandment of love, in greater harmony and peace.
Lord we pray. **Lord, hear our prayer.**

For those who feel trapped by darkness, or burdened by doubt and insecurity

For unity among Christians so that the world may believe

For those in schools and colleges, that their work may help the world

Let us pray to our Lady, who always responded generously to the word of God. **Hail Mary...**

Let us pray in silence for those wishes that are closest to our hearts.

Celebrant Father, we pray that we may learn always to aks for what is right, through Christ our Lord.

7th SUNDAY OF EASTER

Celebrant As we have been called to share in the Spirit, let us now as God's people together put our requests to the Lord.

Reader We pray for the whole Church, that all may be true to your name; and especially we pray for our holy father the pope, our bishops and our priests.
Lord, in your mercy. **Hear our prayer.**

We pray for a true spirit of unity in our country, and for a proper respect for people of other cultures and creeds.
Lord, in your mercy. **Hear our prayer.**

For farmers, who are anxious about the summer crops

For the victims of violence, that they may be able to forgive

For travellers and all who are on holiday

May Mary, the mother of the Church, be with us now as we say. **Hail Mary...**

Let us pray in silence for the things we cannot put into words.

Celebrant God our Father, it is with fulness of heart that we bring these prayers before you. Help us to accomplish what we pray for by our own efforts, that we may give glory to you through your Son Jesus Christ.

PENTECOST SUNDAY

Celebrant The Spirit of God came to the apostles so that they could speak to the world about the wonderful works of God. Let us pray for that Spirit still to be sent out into the world.

Reader Let us pray that Christians everywhere may recognise the different gifts of the Spirit and know that together they form the one Body of Christ.
Come Holy Spirit. **Fill the hearts of your faithful.**

Let us pray that the Church may live by the Spirit of love, joy, peace, patience, kindness, goodness, trustfulness and gentleness.
Come Holy Spirit. **Fill the hearts of your faithful.**

That those who are not at peace with themselves or their fellow men may find it

That husband and wife, parents and children, friend and friend who have quarrelled may forgive each other

That non-Christians who are searching for God's Spirit may find him

Let us pray that like Mary we may be obedient to the Spirit. **Hail Mary...**

God's Spirit is in our hearts; let us be still and know him.

Celebrant Lord God, you have shown yourself in the power and warmth of your Spirit. Send your Spirit so that all may walk with confidence and humility. We make our prayer through Christ our Lord.

CORPUS CHRISTI

Celebrant The Eucharist is the promise of the future unity of all mankind in the love of Christ. Let us pray for the coming of that day.

Reader We pray that all Christians may be brought into love and communion with each other, and so nourish the world.
We pray to the Lamb of God. **Hear our prayer.**

We pray for those making their first Holy Communion at this time of the year. May they come to appreciate your gift more deeply and never take the Mass for granted.
We pray to the Lamb of God. **Hear our prayer.**

For unity among nations

For those who do not recognise their hunger for the love of God

For the peace of all families, that divisions and misunderstandings may be healed

We pray to the mother of the Church and the mother of all people. It was her consent that formed the body of Jesus. **Hail Mary...**

We pray in silence, knowing that those who ask will receive.

Celebrant Father, may all men be one, as we are one in the Eucharist with you and with each other, through Christ our Lord.

TRINITY SUNDAY

Celebrant We are children of God and can call God our Father. Moved by the Spirit let us pray to him with great confidence.

Reader We pray that Christians, baptised in the name of the Father, the Son and the Holy Spirit, may recognise their common baptism and be united in faith and practice.
In your mercy, Lord. **Hear our prayer.**

We pray that men everywhere may come to know the goodness of the living God and keep his law.
In your mercy, Lord. **Hear our prayer.**

For those whose family life is unhappy

For those who are unsure of their faith in God

For those whose work brings them close to the things of creation

Let us pray that like Mary we may be obedient to the Father. **Hail Mary...**

God speaks to us in silence; let us listen to him.

Celebrant Lord God, you have shown yourself as Father, Son and Spirit. We pray to you knowing that all truth and goodness are in you. We make our prayer through your Son, Jesus Christ our Lord.

THE SACRED HEART

Celebrant Christ, by his life and death, shows us how God loves us. The symbol of his heart, pierced by the soldier's lance, expresses this love without limit. Confidently we put our needs before the God who loves us.

Reader We pray that the Church may have a deeper and stronger trust in Jesus, who brings mankind the forgiveness and love of his Father, so that it may never doubt his love.

Let us see, O Lord, your mercy. **And grant us your saving help.**

We pray that all Christians may trustfully answer the invitation of Jesus, who invites them to share the love and desires of his human heart.

Let us see, O Lord, your mercy. **And grant us your saving help.**

For the suffering members of the Church

For those who have lost hope and love

For peace throughout the world

May Mary, who stood by the cross of Christ and shared his love and sacrifice, support our prayers. **Hail Mary...**

Let us ask the compassionate heart of Christ for what we need.

Celebrant Loving Father, you show us the human heart of your Son, loving your people with a human love. Help us to overcome our lack of love for others. We make our prayer through the same Jesus Christ our Lord.

1st SUNDAY IN ORDINARY TIME

The Baptism of Our Lord

Celebrant God calls us to bring true justice on the earth. We pray for the needs of a tormented world.

Reader We pray for the persecuted, for those in concentration camps and for those who suffer for conscience's sake and for the cause of right.
Hear us, O Lord. **And answer our prayers.**

We pray for disarmament, that nations may spend their wealth on the provision of a better life for all nations.
Hear us, O Lord. **And answer our prayers.**

For the abolition of all forms of slave labour

For a genuine and non-partisan approach to politics

For vocations to the service of the ministry

Mary allowed Jesus to leave home to do God's work. May she help us to leave whatever hinders our following of her Son, as we pray. **Hail Mary...**

Let us bring to the Father our needs and worries, in quiet prayer.

Celebrant Lord, through science and technology you teach us to tap the riches of the earth. Help us, we pray, to share your gifts with all nations. We make our prayer through Christ our Lord.

2nd SUNDAY IN ORDINARY TIME

Celebrant Samuel was helped by Eli to know when God was speaking to him; the first disciples were helped by John the Baptist to recognise Jesus as the promised Saviour. Let us pray for all those whose task it is to lead others to God.

Reader That all priests, parents and teachers may learn to recognise God's word in their own lives, so that they can in turn help those entrusted to them, we pray to the Lord.
Speak to us Lord. **That we may hear your word.**

That the Church may understand God's way of speaking, and be open to hearing his word from the most unexpected sources, we pray to the Lord.
Speak to us Lord. **That we may hear your word.**

That all may come to a deeper understanding of the meaning of the Incarnation

That all those who ask for our help will not go disappointed

That the sick and the poor will have the Gospel preached to them

Let us ask Mary, who heard the word of God and kept it, to pray with us. **Hail Mary...**

It was in the silence of the night, and of the desert that Samuel and John heard the voice of God. Let us, too, in silence listen and respond to his word.

Celebrant God our Father, you do not ask for sacrifice and offerings, but an open ear. Let us come to you in simplicity and poverty, not trusting in our own strength, but open to your healing word. We ask this through Jesus, your Son and Word.

3rd SUNDAY IN ORDINARY TIME

Celebrant God has called Christians to know Christ and to help others to know him. Their actions and words are to show what he asks of his followers: unselfishness, generosity and forgiveness. Let us ask God that his Spirit will enable them to do this.

Reader We pray for all Christians. May the example of Jesus who lived on earth as a man and showed people how to live encourage them now to follow the guidance of his spirit.
Lord, in your mercy. **Hear our prayer.**

We pray for those who do not know Jesus Christ. May the love and concern of Christians help them to find him.
Lord, in your mercy. **Hear our prayer.**

For those who are answering God's call with generosity

For those preparing to be priests

For peace in the world

Let us ask Mary, who responded with her whole heart to the call of God, to present our prayers to God.
Hail Mary...

Let us make our own prayers to God who has called us.

Celebrant Father, make your people understand better what you ask of them as members of your family, the Church, and help them to respond when Jesus says 'Follow me'. We ask this through the same Jesus Christ our Lord.

4th SUNDAY IN ORDINARY TIME

Celebrant We have listened to the Word of God. Christ has spoken to us with authority through the Church. We now approach God our Father in the name of Christ with hope and trust.

Reader For all those who are prevented from hearing the Word of God, through material circumstances or their own disposition, we pray to the Lord.
God of life. **Hear our prayer.**

For all Christians who afraid or unable to speak the Word of God, through oppression or lack of understanding, we pray to the Lord.
God of life. **Hear our prayer.**

For teachers and catechists

For the lonely, the depressed and the fearful

For those who love us

Mary responded to God with trust throughout her life. In the same spirit we ask her to pray for us. **Hail Mary...**

Let us pray for a moment in silence.

Celebrant Heavenly Father, you save us through the teaching of your risen Son and the power of your Holy Spirit. Hear the prayers we make to you, who are God for ever and ever.

5th SUNDAY IN ORDINARY TIME

Celebrant Jesus cured the sick and brought comfort and meaning into the lives of many. Let us pray for those who need his comfort now.

Reader For those who are restless and whose lives seem to be without meaning, we pray to the Lord.
Hear us, O Lord. **Hear us, O Lord.**

For those who suffer without deserving to, those who endure pain inflicted through no fault of their own, we pray to the Lord.
Hear us, O Lord. **Hear us, O Lord.**

For those who fill their emptiness with noise and entertainment

For those shattered by unexpected grief

For those who turn to us for comfort and support

We seek the comfort of a mother's help as we say. **Hail Mary...**

Now for a few moments we invite God into the secret of our lives that he may bring us peace.

Celebrant God the Father, creator of heaven and earth, guide your people through the darkness of their lives to that peace which only you can bring, through Christ our Lord.

6th SUNDAY IN ORDINARY TIME

Celebrant Let us call upon Jesus, who never refused to help, and ask him to help all those most in need in the world today.

Reader For all who are sick in mind or body, that Jesus' power and compassion may bring them strength and joy, we pray to the Lord.
Lord, hear us. **Lord, graciously hear us.**

For all who are deprived of a source of knowledge, that Jesus may guide them to his Father, we pray to the Lord.
Lord, hear us. **Lord, graciously hear us.**

For lepers and outcasts, and for those whose sins have made them repulsive

For those who care for the unwanted; for those who listen patiently

For those who suffer from the cold

Let us ask Mary, the mother who suffered with her Son, to pray for all her suffering children. **Hail Mary...**

Let us listen in silence to those who cry for help.

Celebrant Lord God, you sent your Son to heal the wounds of the world. Look with pity on those who suffer today in so many different ways, and hear the prayers we make for them, through Christ your Son, our Lord.

7th SUNDAY IN ORDINARY TIME

Celebrant God is our hope. He offers us forgiveness as soon as we turn back to him, provided we also forgive those who trespass against us. We turn to him now with our requests.

Reader We pray for all those who are not aware of their own sinfulness, that they may repent and be converted.
In your mercy, Lord. **Hear our prayer.**

We pray for those who are not quick to forgive others, that they may remember to be reconciled to their brother before coming to the altar to worship.
In your mercy, Lord. **Hear our prayer.**

For those who think they cannot be forgiven

For those tempted to commit suicide

For those in authority

Let us ask the prayers of Mary who was without sin.
Hail Mary...

Let us pray for a moment in silence, asking God for his forgiving love.

Celebrant Father, you reconcile us to yourself through your Son Jesus Christ. As we share this Eucharist together, we associate ourselves with him and with each other, begging pardon from you and from those we have offended. We make this prayer through Jesus Christ our Lord.

8th SUNDAY IN ORDINARY TIME

Celebrant God loves his people as a husband loves his bride. Let us turn to him now and pray.

Reader Let us pray for those who are faced with new difficulties in their lives. May they have the courage to face them without losing heart.
Lord, we pray. **Lord, hear our prayer.**

Let us pray for those who are bound up with ideas and principles. May they always make persons their concern.
Lord, we pray. **Lord, hear our prayer.**

For those responsible for the Church in changing times

For those who are hurt by change

For those who suffer through revolutions and civil war

Let us ask Mary to pray with us. **Hail Mary...**

Let us pray for a moment about our own uncertainties for the future.

Celebrant Father, you live beyond all change; look on our unstable world and hear our prayers through Jesus Christ, the beginning and end of all things.

9th SUNDAY IN ORDINARY TIME

Celebrant Let us now speak to God our Father from our hearts, and not just with our lips, as we pray together for the needs of mankind.

Reader Let us pray for those whose task it is to implement the law. May they use it in a right spirit and in the cause of freedom.
Lord, hear us. **Lord, graciously hear us.**

Let us pray for those whose weakness and failings lead them to break the law. May they trust in your commandment of love and find strength.
Lord, hear us. **Lord, graciously hear us.**

For those who are depressed and suffering from mental illness

For those who make this world a happier place

For servers and choirs who help the liturgy to be celebrated with devotion and reverence

We now join our prayers to our Lady's. **Hail Mary...**

For a few moments let us speak to the Lord in the silence of our hearts.

Celebrant Father, listen to our prayers, those both spoken and unspoken, which we offer to you through Christ our Lord.

10th SUNDAY IN ORDINARY TIME

Celebrant Following in Adam's footsteps, all are faced with temptation every day of their lives. With this in mind let us pray:

Reader That all Christians, united with Christ in his Church, may stand firm in times of trial, whether of mind or body, we pray to the Lord.
Lord, hear us. **Lord, graciously hear us.**

That those who are tempted to discriminate against others, on grounds of colour, race, sex, creed or age, may be converted to fight against injustice, we pray to the Lord.
Lord, hear us. **Lord, graciously hear us.**

For those struggling to pray

For those persecuted for their beliefs

For those suffering physically or mentally

Let us ask Mary, the comforter of those who mourn, to teach us how to overcome evil by good. **Hail Mary...**

Let us pray in silence for a while.

Celebrant Father, hear our prayer and strengthen us in our resolve, through Christ our Lord.

11th SUNDAY IN ORDINARY TIME

Celebrant The kingdom of God can grow only if we pray. Therefore we turn to the Lord and say: Lord, in your mercy, hear our prayer.

Reader We pray for the Church, a seed sown in the apparent failure of the cross. May it continue to grow and flourish under the guidance of the pope and bishops, so as to reach the glory of the resurrection.
Lord, in your mercy. **Hear our prayer.**

We pray for the members of other Christian Churches, who strive to know and follow the will of God. May all be united in the worship of the one true God.
Lord, in your mercy. **Hear our prayer.**

For peace, harmony and a common sense of purpose in industry

For sorrow for sins committed through racial intolerance and misunderstanding

For faith and hope for those in shock over the death of a loved one

Let us pray to Mary, that the kingdom of her Son may grow and flourish. **Hail Mary...**

In a moment's quiet prayer let us turn to the Lord.

Celebrant Lord God, we praise you for your kingdom, growing out of the wood of the cross. Grant that by faith and good works that kingdom may increase and multiply. We ask this through Christ our Lord.

12th SUNDAY IN ORDINARY TIME

Celebrant Let us pray to God who is our strength and the source of all hope on behalf of the Church and the world.

Reader Let us pray to the Lord that the troubles and restlessness of the world may be stilled, and all things be made new.
Merciful Lord. **Hear our prayer.**

Let us pray to the Lord that he who calmed the waters may bring peace and calm to the hearts of his people.
Merciful Lord. **Hear our prayer.**

That different cultures may be tolerant of one another

That the suffering members of the Church may draw strength from the example of Christ

That people may recognise the one God and put aside the false gods of fame and fortune

Let us seek the help of our Lady who remained at peace even though a sword pierced her heart. **Hail Mary...**

Let us be quiet and calm for a few moments and listen to God.

Celebrant O God, whose faithfulness lasts for ever, help us in our trials and troubles and grant our requests, through Christ our Lord.

13th SUNDAY IN ORDINARY TIME

Celebrant We remember how generous the Lord Jesus is to us, and in his name we pray to the Father.

Reader For the Church all over the world, that it may be an instrument of God's healing power, bringing hope and life to all men, we pray to the Lord.
Lord, hear us. **Lord, graciously hear us.**

That the peace of Christ will flood the hearts and minds of all those who are haunted by their past, dissatisfied with the present, or afraid of the future, we pray to the Lord.
Lord, hear us. **Lord, graciously hear us.**

For those laid low by sickness of body, illness of mind, or emptiness of heart

For those hoping for the gift of children, and those who have adopted or fostered children

For those who have received special talents

In union with the whole Church we honour our Lady and seek to pray with her. **Hail Mary...**

In a few moments of silence we speak to God of those things nearest our hearts.

Celebrant Lord God, help us your people to work for all the things we dare to pray for, through Jesus Christ your Son.

14th SUNDAY IN ORDINARY TIME

Celebrant The Father has sent his Son to show us the path of life. Let us pray that all people may receive the grace to welcome his teaching and let it change their lives.

Reader That each member of the Church may hear our Lord's call to repentance and belief, and may answer gladly, we pray to the Lord.
May all hear your word. **And follow it.**

That in times of temptation and weakness Christians may never lose confidence in the compassion and grace of God, we pray to the Lord.
May all hear your word. **And follow it.**

For those who suffer in the darkness of unbelief

For bishops, priests and lay people, that they may be courageous in bearing witness to Christ in an age of indifference.

For all who need the healing touch of God's mercy in their lives

That Mary, who welcomed and cherished the word of God, may intercede for us. **Hail Mary...**

In a moment of stillness let us turn our hearts and minds to God.

Celebrant God our Father, you sent your Son Jesus Christ to teach us and lead us. May your people today listen to his word and live in his saving grace. We ask this through the same Christ our Lord.

15th SUNDAY IN ORDINARY TIME

Celebrant Each of us has a place in God's plan from all eternity. Let us ask God for the grace to fulfil the mission he has given his Church.

Reader We pray for the Church throughout the world, especially for our Holy Father, and all leaders of Christian people, that they may be faithful to their mission of leadership in the Church.
Lord, hear your people. **Lord, hear your people.**

We pray for all families, especially fathers and mothers, that they may lead their children to love God as mature Christian adults.
Lord, hear your people. **Lord, hear your people.**

For all foster parents

For the victims of racial prejudice

For the sick and the dying

Let us ask our Lady, the queen of the apostles, to pray with us as we say. **Hail Mary...**

Let us pause for a moment in silence to pray to the God who has given us our tasks.

Celebrant Father, we have listened to the message of your truth. Strengthen our hope in Christ your Son so that we may work to build his kingdom on earth. We make our prayer through Christ our Lord.

16th SUNDAY IN ORDINARY TIME

Celebrant The Lord is my shepherd, there is nothing I shall want. Let us now pray to the Lord and put our trust in him.

Reader We pray that God will watch over, protect and guide the Church, especially the pope, our bishops and all who have ministries of service.
Lord, hear us. **Lord, graciously hear us.**

We pray that all married couples will find in their vocation a true response to the invitation of Christ to love one another.
Lord, hear us. **Lord, graciously hear us.**

For leaders in commerce and industry

For candidates for the priesthood and religious life.

For the families of the victims of murder and assassination

May Mary, the mother of the Church, guide us as we pray together. **Hail Mary...**

Let us pray for a moment in silence.

Celebrant Almighty God and Father, we pray that you will always take pity on us and be our shepherd and our king. We ask this through Christ our Lord.

17th SUNDAY IN ORDINARY TIME

Celebrant Christ our Lord has taught us to pray for our daily bread. Let us consider what this means and pray for the basic needs of all mankind.

Reader For God's people gathered round their pastors at the Eucharistic feast: may no one leave the celebration empty-handed.
Lord, we pray. **Lord, hear our prayer.**

For individuals and nations, that all may show a greater willingness to share their bread with those who have less, or none.
Lord, we pray. **Lord, hear our prayer.**

For employers and employees, that all may be just and honest

For the well-being of parish communities

For peace throughout the world

Let us pray with our Lady who attended to the daily needs of her Son in their home at Nazareth. **Hail Mary...**

In a moment of silence let us pray for God's will to be done.

Celebrant Father, Christ your Son has taught us to ask in his name for what we seek. We do so now, knowing that he lives and reigns with you for ever and ever.

18th SUNDAY IN ORDINARY TIME

Celebrant The fulness of life is to know the Father and Jesus Christ whom he has sent. Let us pray that the Father and the Son will make themselves known to their people.

Reader We pray that the knowledge and love of Jesus will increase in the Church. May he be the centre of Christian life.
Hear us, O God. **And answer our prayer.**

We pray that the love of the Father for all mankind will show his people how to break down barriers and become truly catholic, universal.
Hear us, O God. **And answer our prayer.**

For those unable to accept Christ's invitation to love him

For our Christian brethren of other Churches

For the pope and the bishops, the servants of the world

Like every mother, Mary taught her Son to love. We ask her to continue her work as mother of God's people.
Hail Mary...

Let us pray in silence for the Father to make his will known to us and to all his people

Celebrant Father, show us your Son and help us to know him, love him, hear him and work with him for the welfare of all peoples. We make our prayer through Christ our Lord.

19th SUNDAY IN ORDINARY TIME

Celebrant Elijah was given food in the desert; the Israelites were fed with manna. Both were given food for their journey. Let us ask Jesus to strengthen his people on their journey through life, with the gift of himself.

Reader That all who feel their own strength to be exhausted may come to see the power of God and trust in the promise of Jesus, we pray to the Lord.
Lord, bread of life. **Hear and answer our prayer**

That all who are tempted to live for themselves may take example from Jesus, who gave himself body and spirit for others, we pray to the Lord.
Lord, bread of life. **Hear and answer our prayer.**

For all who share the living Bread in the Eucharist

For all those who are desperate, and for those who help them

For victims of injustice and exploitation

Mary praised God for filling the hungry with good things. May she pray with us for all who hunger for bread, for love, for justice, for God. **Hail Mary...**

Jesus' food was to do his Father's will. Let us pray in silence that God's will be done.

Celebrant Lord, we bring you our needs and the needs of all our fellow men. Answer our prayers as you see best. We make these prayers through Jesus Christ our Lord.

20th SUNDAY IN ORDINARY TIME

Celebrant Christ invites us to the banquet of the Eucharist which is a promise of eternal life. Let us ask for a more living faith as we meet Christ in this sacrament in which we are nourished by his life.

Reader That all those who are fed with the living bread which is Jesus may show a likeness to his ways in their own lives, we pray to the Lord.
Let us see, O Lord, your mercy. **Lord, have mercy.**

That all those who share at the table of the Eucharist may be more ready to share the needs and happiness of others in their daily lives, we pray to the Lord.
Let us see, O Lord, your mercy. **Lord, have mercy.**

For those who have died, that they may share the eternal life begun in this communion of Christ's body and blood

For unbelievers, that they may come to believe in Christ and in the promise of a life to come

For the lonely and the sick, that they may have warmth and comfort

May Mary, who nourished and cherished the Word made flesh, join her prayers to ours as we say. **Hail Mary...**

Let us pray silently to God who has given us bread from heaven.

Celebrant God our Father, may we be transformed into the likeness of Jesus your Son, who lives with you for ever and ever.

21st SUNDAY IN ORDINARY TIME

Celebrant Let us pray with confidence to the Father through Jesus, the Holy One of God, for the needs of all mankind.

Reader Let us pray for all those who have come to Jesus as disciples. May they become ever firmer in their choice for him, and more faithful in following his way.
Lord, hear us. **Lord, graciously hear us.**

Let us pray for those who have important decisions to make in the near future, that they may be guided by the Spirit who gives wisdom.
Lord, hear us. **Lord, graciously hear us.**

For those who through lack of faith walk no more with Christ

For married couples and those preparing for marriage, that they may be faithful to each other

For those with a vocation to the single life who do not have the support of a religious community

Let us ask Mary, the most faithful follower of her Son, to join her prayer with ours. **Hail Mary...**

Let us ask the Holy Spirit to prompt us in the silence of our hearts to seek those things which lead to eternal life.

Celebrant Father, may your people be ever receptive to the words of your Son, which are Spirit and Life. May they be the guiding motive of their lives. Grant our prayer through the same Christ our Lord.

22nd SUNDAY IN ORDINARY TIME

Celebrant Let us pray to God our Father and seek the help of his Holy Spirit in recognising God's will.

Reader We pray that the Holy Spirit of God may guide those who are uncertain, and bring those who have strayed back to the law of love.
Lord, hear us. **And answer our prayer.**

We pray that those whose decisions influence public attitudes may receive the spirit of wisdom and courage.
Lord, hear us. **And answer our prayer.**

That the poor and underprivileged will find help

That people everywhere will find freedom to worship as they wish

That the government will be guided in its decision-making

We ask the support of Mary, who was always obedient to God's will, in our efforts to follow her Son. **Hail Mary...**

Let us now pray in silence

Celebrant Father, you have given your law to guide your people on their pilgrimage. Keep us all in the wisdom of your Spirit, with your Son, in whose name we make this prayer.

23rd SUNDAY IN ORDINARY TIME

Celebrant The disciples of Jesus were amazed by the signs he gave them. Let us pray that his people today may be a sign to the world.

Reader That the power and knowledge at man's command may be used in service of God and of the whole world, we pray to the Lord.
Hear us, Lord. **And grant our prayer.**

That the techniques of medicine and other achievements of science may lead to a lessening of starvation in the world, we pray to the Lord.
Hear us, Lord. **And grant our prayer.**

That writers, publishers and printers may help people to read and reflect on the word of God

That those who work for harmony in the community may spread understanding

That those responsible for the environment may respect natural beauty

We pray that Mary's intercession will help the voice of Jesus to be heard throughout the world. **Hail Mary...**

Let us pray quietly for all who may look to us for a sign.

Celebrant Heavenly Father, help your people to use your gifts wisely and generously, so that the world may see in them a reflection of your glory. We make this prayer through Christ our Lord.

24th SUNDAY IN ORDINARY TIME

Celebrant Christ willingly accepted the sufferings of his life and the agony of his death to open the way to life to us. Let us pray that his people will show a similar willingness to accept their crosses in life.

Reader We pray for a spirit of self-sacrifice in the Church, knowing that true followers of our Lord must be willing to lose their life in order to save it.
Lord, in your mercy. **Hear our prayer.**

We pray for courage in the world, knowing that faith can move mountains and that all things are possible to God.
Lord, in your mercy. **Hear our prayer.**

For those who need food and clothing

For courage to accept the responsibility of being a Christian

For confidence that God is with his people in all their trials

Let us ask Mary to help us to stand as she did beside the cross of Jesus. **Hail Mary...**

Silently let us join in spirit with all the sufferers of the world.

Celebrant Lord Jesus Christ, we pray that your people may have the courage to follow in your footsteps and so share in your glory. We make our prayer in your name, Jesus the Lord.

25th SUNDAY IN ORDINARY TIME

Celebrant Our heavenly Father desires mankind to work for peace and harmony. Let us pray for his help.

Reader We pray for a spirit of truth and generosity among Christians, so that they will encourage peace by honest appreciation of others.
Lord, hear our prayer. **Lord, hear our prayer.**

We pray for the people living in war-torn countries and ask God to help them come to a lasting settlement of their problems.
Lord, hear our prayer. **Lord, hear our prayer.**

For families, that God's love will be mediated, and peace and happiness shared

For different races and creeds that they may recognise their common brotherhood

For those who through entertainment try to bring people together

Let us ask Mary to join us in our prayer for peace.
Hail Mary...

Let us pause and quietly ask God's forgiveness for the dissension in the world.

Celebrant Heavenly Father, help us to understand that we can do nothing without your help. Inspire us in our daily lives, so that we will bring your peace to all we meet. We make our prayer through Christ our Lord.

26th SUNDAY IN ORDINARY TIME

Celebrant God's Spirit has come to the world, though many reject this spirit because of the hardness of their hearts. Let us pray that men may be open to his gifts.

Reader Let us pray that Christians may hear the prophetic voice of God's Spirit wherever it sounds and read the signs of our own times.
Lord, hear our call. **Lord, hear our call.**

Let us pray that men and women may see more clearly the inequality and injustice of the world, and be prepared to live in greater simplicity and poverty, for the well-being of others.
Lord, hear our call. **Lord, hear our call.**

For the starving and those who work for them

For those who work in industrial relations

For Church leaders

Mary's life was prophecy, poverty and charity. Let us ask for her help. **Hail Mary...**

Let us pray silently for our own intentions.

Celebrant Father, you call us through your word in the scriptures and through your Spirit in the world. Grant us the grace to hear and see you wherever you are, through Jesus Christ our Lord.

27th SUNDAY IN ORDINARY TIME

Celebrant We turn in prayer to the Father whose will it is that his children should live happily together in harmony and peace.

Reader For married people, that they may grow in happiness and in love for one another, let us pray to the Lord.
In your mercy, Lord. **Hear our prayer.**

For those who have suffered much in their lives, that God may give them relief, patience and joy, we pray to the Lord.
In your mercy, Lord. **Hear our prayer.**

For children to sense God's love for them through the love of their parents

For broken families and those who try to help them

For psychiatrists and counsellors, and those who consult them

Let us ask the mother of Jesus to pray for us. **Hail Mary...**

Let us approach God trustfully in silence.

Celebrant Father, however faithless your people, you are always faithful. May the Spirit of Jesus keep us true to those you have given us to love. We ask this in the name of Jesus Christ our Lord.

28th SUNDAY IN ORDINARY TIME

Celebrant The rich young man turned away from Jesus because he felt too much had been asked of him. Let us pray for a spirit of courage and response in people today.

Reader We pray for those to whom God has given beauty, riches and deep feelings, that they may not waste their gifts, but use them wisely to give joy to those who have nothing.
Lord, hear us. **Lord, graciously hear us.**

Let us pray for those who are working to preserve the beauties of creation for man's enrichment.
Lord, hear us. **Lord, graciously hear us.**

For all refugees, wanderers, and homesick people

For those in mental homes

For those who abuse God's gifts

We now ask Mary, who cared for our Lord, to teach us to care for all who are entrusted to us. **Hail Mary...**

For a few moments now let us put our thoughts before God in silence.

Celebrant Father, may your people respond to your Son's call to follow him, and never hold back. We make this prayer in his name, Jesus the Lord.

29th SUNDAY IN ORDINARY TIME

Celebrant Christ said that anyone who wants to become great must first of all become a servant. Let us then pray that all his people may learn to be humble.

Reader We pray that Christians may learn to show their love of God in humble service of others.
Lord, hear our prayer. **And let our cry come to you.**

We pray that all those in positions of authority may see their task as service to those less able to influence the course of their lives.
Lord, hear our prayer. **And let our cry come to you.**

That politicians and economists may plan in human terms

That persecutors and their victims may be reconciled

That men and women may find peace within themselves and with each other

We pray that our Lady will help all to greater generosity in the service of her Son. **Hail Mary...**

Let us pray in silence for our own intentions.

Celebrant Lord, it is only through your grace that your people can live as you would have them live. Grant that this grace may never be lacking, through Christ our Lord.

30th SUNDAY IN ORDINARY TIME

Celebrant In the knowledge that God is the Father of mercies and the giver of all consolation, let us turn to him once again in Jesus's name, and ask him to comfort his people.

Reader Let us pray to the Lord that he will show himself to his people, so that they may know him as their God and find strength in his presence.
Lord, in your mercy. **Hear our prayer.**

Let us pray to the Lord to make the light of his truth shine on his people, so that the cloud of ignorance may be lifted from their minds and their prejudices removed.
Lord, in your mercy. **Hear our prayer.**

For those who are physically blind, and those who work for them

For those who have been baptised recently

For those whose work is dull, monotonous and laborious

The saving faith which Jesus praised in Bartimaeus, is seen most of all in Mary. Let us now pray to her. **Hail Mary...**

In quietness let us seek the Lord.

Celebrant Lord God, you have called us from darkness into your own great light. Do not allow us to be blinded by falsehood, prejudice or intolerance, but continue to guide us graciously by your Holy Spirit, through Christ our Lord.

31st SUNDAY IN ORDINARY TIME

Celebrant Needing God's love above all things we turn to him and pray that his love for his Church and the world will never fail.

Reader Let us pray that God's love and mercy be reflected in his Church, especially when its members are gathered to celebrate the Eucharist.
Lord, hear our prayer. **And let our cry come to you.**

Let us pray that all Christians may be freed from prejudice and learn to love all their fellows because they are children of God.
Lord, hear our prayer. **And let our cry come to you.**

For the mentally handicapped

For family and friends

For the unemployed and their families

Mary knew what it is to love, in good times and in bad. Let us therefore pray to her and say. **Hail Mary...**

Love speaks in silence; so let us listen to God in our hearts.

Celebrant God our Father, your love for us is shown in the death and resurrection of your Son. Help us to be like him and live for others. We ask this in his name, Jesus Christ our Lord.

32nd SUNDAY IN ORDINARY TIME

Celebrant We ask for the confidence to place the needs of the Church and the world before God. For this we pray to the Lord: Lord, hear our prayer.

Reader We pray that the Church may be the body of Christ, the new Temple, through its members giving unstintingly of themselves, recognizing their dependence on the Father, who is the source of all good.
Let us pray to the Lord. **Lord, hear our prayer.**

We pray that those in positions of authority may willingly follow the example of our Lord by being whole-hearted in the service of others.
Let us pray to the Lord. **Lord, hear our prayer.**

That married couples may be blessed with a life of harmony

That the homeless may find a dwelling place worthy of human dignity

That the sick may look on the passion of Christ and so find strength

Let us pray to Mary who relied completely on God.
Hail Mary...

Let us now pray quietly for our own intentions.

Celebrant Father, help your people to walk in light and give encouragement to those they meet, so that your Church may grow, through Christ our Lord.

33rd SUNDAY IN ORDINARY TIME

Celebrant Because we know neither the day nor the hour, we stand ready in prayer.

Reader That the Church in all its institutions and works, in all its teachings and proclamations, will show forth God's love and forgiveness for all men, we pray to the Lord.
In your mercy, Lord. **Hear our prayer.**

That all our fellow Christians, our Jewish friends, and those of other faiths or none may be united in openness of mind and heart, we pray to the Lord.
In your mercy, Lord. **Hear our prayer.**

For those who suffer at the hands of violent men, institutions and governments

For those in prison, that they may not lose faith in themselves or in their fellow men

That those with ageing relatives and friends may not neglect them

We seek the prayer of our Lady for all those we know and love. **Hail Mary...**

In a few moments of silence we open our hearts to God.

Celebrant Lord, you know each of us by name; may we always hear whenever you call. We make our prayer through Christ our Lord.

34th SUNDAY IN ORDINARY TIME

Christ the King

Celebrant Christ our Lord, the King of kings, brings us into his kingdom and presents us to the Father. In, through and with his Son, let us pray for his kingdom to come.

Reader That the whole Church may remain faithful in its witness, as Jesus Christ its head is faithful, we pray to the Lord.
Lord, may your kingdom come. **On earth as in heaven.**

That voice of Christ the King may ring out through the world, calling all to hear his truth and live according to his message, we pray to the Lord.
Lord, may your kingdom come. **On earth as in heaven.**

For those in authority, that they may learn from Christ the King

For those who have sinned, that they may grow in sorrow

For the wealthy, that they may be poor in spirit

Mary listened to the truth and pondered on it in her heart. May she now enrich us by her prayer. **Hail Mary...**

In silent prayer and unwavering hope let us await the generosity of God.

Celebrant Father in heaven, give your people the grace they need to flourish in your Son's kingdom, and to worship you in spirit and in truth. We make our prayer through him who is king for ever.

1st SUNDAY OF ADVENT

Celebrant God sent his Son into the world to save it from sin. Let us pray that his people who now look forward to the feast of his birth may carry on his work of taking away the sin of the world.

Reader We pray for God's people, the Church, that it may be filled with the Holy Spirit of the Redeemer whose coming it awaits.
Lord, be with your people. **Now and forever.**

We pray for the world God loved so much, that a spirit of prayer and waiting on God may prevail in these troubled times.
Lord, be with your people. **Now and forever.**

For those who lack patience and trust

For those whose lives make it hard for them to feel God's love

For all who are sad, and who feel that God has turned his face away from them

Mary was aware of her own poverty and emptiness, and therefore God was able to fill her with the Holy Spirit. Let us ask her to help us to have the same openness to God. **Hail Mary...**

Let us open ourselves to God in silence, confident that he knows what is in our hearts.

Celebrant Father of Jesus, and our Father, give us the Spirit of your Son, so that the feast of his birthday may be for us a new beginning. We ask this for his sake, Jesus Christ the Lord.

2nd SUNDAY OF ADVENT

Celebrant John the Baptist came to prepare people for the coming of Christ. Let us respond in prayer to the word of God as our preparation for the coming of Christ.

Reader We pray for Christians gathered in their local communities throughout the world, that this Advent may be a time of nourishment and transformation for them.
We pray together. **Come, Lord Jesus, come.**

We pray for the pope, our bishops and priests, that their faithfulness to Christ's message may bring greater freedom and peace to the world.
We pray together. **Come, Lord Jesus, come.**

For those who are afraid of dying

For those young people who find no meaning in life

For those who have no belief

Mary waited patiently for the coming of her Son. Let us ask her to join her prayers to ours at this time of preparation. **Hail Mary...**

Let us now pause for a moment of silent prayer.

Celebrant John the Baptist prepared the way for Jesus by proclaiming a baptism of repentance for the forgiveness of sins. May we become faithful bearers of God's redeeming word as we prepare in word and action for the coming of Christ. We make our prayer through this same Jesus, who is our Lord for ever.

3rd SUNDAY OF ADVENT

Celebrant We are preparing for the coming of Jesus, God's Son. Although we try to make our hearts ready, true readiness lies only in his gift. We pray for the waiting Church and world.

Reader Let us pray that there may grow in the Church a deeper understanding of what the coming of Jesus into the world must mean, of the kind of new creation God wants us to work for.
Lord, hear us. **Lord, graciously hear us.**

Let us pray that the world may come to understand the true meaning of happiness in Christ, and not be led astray by what is on the surface.
Lord, hear us. **Lord, graciously hear us.**

For those in prison for whatever reason

For those suffering from depression

For those who have died

Mary waited for the birth of Jesus, ready to accept whatever God should ask of her. Let us ask her help in our preparation for Christmas. **Hail Mary...**

Let us pray for those needs which we keep locked up in our own hearts.

Celebrant Father of Jesus and of all mankind, stretch out your hand and save your people from the mistakes and evils which are in us and around us. We ask this in the name of Jesus the Lord.

4th SUNDAY OF ADVENT

Celebrant Mary's humility made her accept to be the mother of our Saviour. Let us pray that Christians today may share that same spirit of humility so as to prepare for the coming of our Lord.

Reader We pray for the universal Church, that all members of the Church may provide a home for Christ on earth.
Lord, in your mercy. **Hear our prayer.**

We pray for Christians everywhere, that their lives may be such that Christ can enter in.
Lord, in your mercy. **Hear our prayer.**

For the homeless in this country

For the Jews, whose religious heritage we share

For those who are lonely and forgotten

Using the words of Gabriel let us pray to become more like Mary. **Hail Mary...**

Let us pray in silence for the coming of Jesus among us.

Celebrant Father, it was by your will and by the work of the Spirit that Mary became the mother of your Son. Send down upon us that same Spirit so that we may give birth to Jesus Christ in our hearts. We ask this in his name, Jesus the Lord.

CHRISTMAS: DAWN MASS

Celebrant With Mary, Joseph and the shepherds we rejoice at the birth of our Saviour, and through him offer our prayers on behalf of all men.

Reader Let us pray for all those who are ignored or forgotten. May they come to find love and acceptance in the universal Fatherhood of God.
Lord, hear us. **Lord, graciously hear us.**

Let us pray for those who no longer have the support of a family about them, and for those who have never known the warmth of family affection.
Lord, hear us. **Lord, graciously hear us.**

For minorities, separated from others by differences of race, religion or language

For peace between nations, especially in troubled areas

For the dead, that they may share the new birth that this feast proclaims

Let us ask Mary the mother of Jesus and our mother to join her prayer with ours. **Hail Mary...**

Let us pray in the peace and stillness of our own hearts.

Celebrant Father, may Christ be born again in his people by faith and love, and may his light continue to shine among them and bring them to you. Grant this prayer through the same Jesus Christ our Lord.

(Prayers for Midnight Mass are on p. 55, and for the Midday Mass on p. 181.)

HOLY FAMILY

(1st Sunday after Christmas)

Celebrant It was the Father's will that his Son should share in our humanity and enjoy a genuine family life. On this feast of the Holy Family we ask him to comfort and nourish families everywhere with his love.

Reader We pray that the family of the Church may grow in wisdom and in grace.
Lord, bless your family. **Lord, bless your people.**

We pray that all God's people who are parents, sons or daughters, may come to a deeper love and understanding of one another.
Lord, bless your family. **Lord, bless your people.**

For our own families with their joys and troubles

For broken families, deserted partners, battered wives, deprived children

For those whose life at home is full of tension, misunderstanding and misery

Mary cared for her Son with a mother's love; she continues to care for his Church, and so we say. **Hail Mary...**

We are God's family, his very sons and daughters. In the intimacy of silent prayer let us confide in him.

Celebrant Father, your saving work makes our scattered human race into a single family. May this day's celebration bring that saving work still nearer its completion. Through Christ our Lord.

THE OCTAVE OF CHRISTMAS

The Solemnity of Mary, Mother of God

Celebrant Mary recognised God's action in the birth of her Son. She treasured what happened and pondered it in her heart. Let us ask God to make his work known today.

Reader Let us pray for all married people, that the whole community may help, support and encourage them.
Lord, hear us. **Hear our prayer**

Let us pray for parents and their children, that they may show understanding and patience to each other and grow together in confidence and hope.
Lord, hear us. **Hear our prayer.**

For single people, that God will give them good friends

For teachers, that they will be refreshed for their self-giving work

For young people, that they may work for a better world

We pray to Mary, the model of wives, mothers and teachers. **Hail Mary...**

In our silence let us invite God to speak to us and show us his will.

Celebrant Father, you gave everything to your Son who shared everything with his friends. May we also be humble enough to receive and generous enough to share. Through Christ our Lord.

2nd SUNDAY AFTER CHRISTMAS

Celebrant We can know God only through Jesus, who was born into our world and lived a human life. Let us pray that the light of Jesus will show the world the way to God.

Reader We pray for the Church, that it may not seek earthly glory, but proclaim humility and self-sacrifice, especially by its own example.
Lord, in your mercy. **Hear our prayer**

We pray for all God's people, that they may acknowledge the Father in truth and serve him in holiness.
Lord, in your mercy. **Hear our prayer.**

For those who rule nations, that God's Spirit may enter into their hearts

For the bishops, that they may work together

For Christians, that they may witness to Jesus by their lives

Let us ask Mary, mother of Jesus, to present our prayers to her Son. **Hail Mary..**

Let us pray silently for what we need.

Celebrant God our Father, unite all those who bear the name of Christian, that the world may believe in Jesus Christ whom you have sent.

THE EPIPHANY

Celebrant Today we celebrate the revelation of the Son of God to the whole world. Let us pray that people everywhere will come to recognise him.

Reader Let us pray for the poor and needy of the world, that Jesus may be seen in them and justice done to them.
Lord, hear our prayer. **And show us your mercy.**

Let us pray for missionaries, that the growth of the Church through their efforts may give them encouragement and inspiration in their work of spreading the Gospel.
Lord, hear our prayer. **And show us your mercy.**

For statesmen and diplomats, that they may work with honesty and integrity

For those who work in industry, that they may work for industrial peace with justice

For all those in public life, that they may not compromise Christian principles

Let us ask Mary, the mother of Jesus Christ, our Lord and Saviour, to pray for us. **Hail Mary...**

Let us pray in silence that Jesus may be revealed to us.

Celebrant Father, you show us your Son, and continue his work among us in the power of the Holy Spirit. May we and all his people be faithful co-workers with the Spirit. We ask this in the name of Jesus, your Son.

ASH WEDNESDAY

Celebrant We are reminded when we are signed with the ashes that we are but dust. Let us pray that this summons to repentance may be heard by all Christians.

Reader We pray that this period of Lent may be one of honesty for all Christians, in solidarity with our Lord and inspired by his love.
Lord, hear us. **Lord, graciously hear us.**

We pray for all those for whom fasting is their daily lot, whether they wish it or not, that they may receive a fairer share of the world's resources.
Lord, hear us. **Lord, graciously hear us.**

We pray for all those who are making a special effort to overcome some fault. May the Lord be with them and help them.
Lord, hear us. **Lord, graciously hear us.**

For those whose office is to give a lead in the Church

For those whose handicaps prevent them from playing an active part

Let us share our time of prayer with Mary, the mother of our Saviour. **Hail Mary...**

We must spend time in the desert if we are to know God. Let us be with him now in silence.

Celebrant Father, your Son was led by the Spirit into the desert. We pray that his people may be driven by the same Spirit to watch and pray, so that they may not enter into temptation. We make our prayer through Christ Jesus our Lord.

1st SUNDAY OF LENT

Celebrant Let us pray that the words of the Scriptures we have listened to may help to bring all Christian people to repentance and renewal.

Reader We pray for the Church, that all its members may come through penance to a greater understanding of the Good News and a renewed strength to spread it throughout the world.
Hear us, O Lord. **And answer our prayer.**

We pray for all those whose hearts are still hardeneed, that they may find enlightenment during this time of preparation for Easter and emerge from it with a new spirit.
Hear us, O Lord. **And answer our prayer.**

For catechists, who proclaim God's word

For parents, that they may be patient with their children

For those who live in the wilderness without hope

Let us ask Mary to help us listen to her Son. **Hail Mary...**

For a moment let us listen to the Spirit in our hearts.

Celebrant Father, you have given your people a second birth in baptism. Bring to birth in each of us the love we would like to have for each other. We make our prayer through Christ our Lord.

2nd SUNDAY OF LENT

Celebrant With God on our side, who can be against us? With great confidence let us call upon God in prayer.

Reader We pray that with the Spirit of God comforting the Church, its members will go out into the world strengthened and be seen as disciples of Christ.
Lord, hear us. **Lord, graciously hear us.**

We pray that all Christians will have the wisdom to know God's will and the spirit to obey it as faithfully as Abraham.
Lord, hear us. **Lord, graciously hear us.**

For those who are starving

For those who are fighting against God's will

For the Church in this parish

Let us ask Mary to pray with us. **Hail Mary...**

Let us in silence remember all those for whom we have promised to pray.

Celebrant Lord Jesus, you are close to us always, and know our true needs. May we stay in your presence, listen to you, and welcome your Spirit. We make our prayer in your name, Jesus our Lord and God.

3rd SUNDAY OF LENT

Celebrant We are all sanctuaries of God's presence. Let us pray that people throughout the world will be treated with respect and understanding.

Reader We pray that as Christ was strongest in the weakness of his passion, so may his strength be seen in those who are crucified by hardship and oppression today.
Hear us, O Lord. **And answer our prayer.**

We pray that as God's commandments are for all time, so may the rulers of nations come to see them as the only lasting basis for peace.
Hear us, O Lord. **And answer our prayer.**

For those who do not see the need for prayer

For those who do not like participating in the liturgy

For those who know God's will but are afraid to do it

Let us ask Mary to pray that all may enjoy the freedom that comes from keeping God's law. **Hail Mary...**

Let us wait in silence for God to speak to us.

Celebrant Lord Jesus Christ, you know your people's weakness and their tendency to sin. Comfort them with your presence and give them the energy to work for good. We make our prayer in your name, Jesus the Lord.

4th SUNDAY OF LENT

Celebrant God so loved the world that he gave his only Son, so that everyone who believes in him may live. Let us now, confident in God's love, pray for the world he loved.

Reader We pray that those who are living in the dark may see the light who is Christ, and learn to believe that God is love.
Lord, hear us. **Lord, graciously hear us.**

We pray for the unemployed and for their families. May they be given the strength to meet their hardships with hope.
Lord, hear us. **Lord, graciously hear us.**

For those who are blind, and those who work with them

For prisoners of conscience

For those responsible for the resources of the earth

We ask Mary to pray for us that we may learn to love her Son more. **Hail Mary...**

Let us now pray in silence to the God who is love.

Celebrant God our Father, look with love on all your children. May they never forget your constant care for them and the promise of your forgiveness, made known to us through Christ our Lord.

5th SUNDAY OF LENT

Celebrant Let us pray with confidence to God, since his care for his people is without limit, saying: Lord, our God. Hear our prayer.

Reader That the Church of God may learn to let go of what is less important, grasp what is of real value, and so yield a rich harvest, we pray to the Lord.
Lord, our God. **Hear our prayer.**

That Christians may be the first to break down barriers and replace them with reconciliation and new life, we pray to the Lord.
Lord, our God. **Hear our prayer.**

That the Church may grow in love and unity

That those who are sick in mind or body may find comfort and healing

That those who have died may enjoy the presence of God for ever

Let us ask Mary to pray for us and all mankind.
Hail Mary...

Let us ask God in silence to grant our prayers.

Celebrant Father, your Son was the grain of wheat that died and bore good fruit. Help us to die to ourselves so that we, too, may learn to love without limit, through Christ our Lord.

6th SUNDAY OF LENT

Passion Sunday

Celebrant We have listened to the story of the Passion of our Lord. With sadness we look at the continued violence and sinfulness of our world. Christ's final words from the cross were of forgiveness, so let us ask God to soften men's hearts as we pray.

Reader We pray for all those who share in Christ's sufferings through their sufferings in the world, that they may find comfort and strength.
We pray to the Lord. **Lord, hear our prayer.**

We pray for those who have the courage and honesty to work openly for justice and peace, that their efforts may be rewarded.
We pray to the Lord. **Lord, hear our prayer.**

For those whose efforts to improve the lives of others are rejected

For peace in the world

For all those who have died, that they may enjoy the happiness of Christ's resurrection

Let us ask Mary, standing at the foot of the cross, to teach men to forgive. **Hail Mary...**

Let us ask God in the silence of our own hearts to grant us his peace.

Celebrant God, our Father, there is much in the world that calls for remorse. Turn our remorse into sorrow, and our sorrow into joy at your forgiveness, which comes to us through Christ our Lord.

MAUNDY THURSDAY

Celebrant Our Lord and Master became the sacrificial Lamb, who lived and died for others. Let us pray that men will live and die following his example. So with him we pray: Father, your will be done.

Reader We pray for the whole Church, the living body of Christ. May the members of this Body always be willing to give themselves generously for the world.
We pray with Christ. **Father, your will be done.**

We pray for the Jewish people, against whom Christians have sinned. May they come to a fulfilment of their hopes, through Jesus, the saviour of the world.
We pray with Christ. **Father, your will be done.**

For those in the agony of a breakdown, that they may find support and encouragement

For the gift of humility, and for those who have found the lowest place

For priests, that they may offer Mass with conviction, and live it in their lives

Tonight, recalling Mary's pain as she prayed for her Son at the hour of his death we ask her to pray with us.
Hail Mary...

Let us pray in silence that we may not be put to the test.

Celebrant Father, you have given us in Jesus an example of perfect love. Teach us this sacrificial love so that nothing will separate us from him who lives with you now and always.

EASTER SUNDAY

Celebrant Let us pray to God, the almighty Father, who raised his Son Jesus from the dead. Let us ask him that all his people may share in the glory of the resurrection.

Reader Let us pray for Christians throughout the world. May they remain true to the new life they received at baptism and live always with the life of the risen Christ.
Lord, in your mercy. **Hear our prayer.**

Let us pray for all those who this Easter have received new life by baptism. May they discover the face of the risen Christ in their new brothers and sisters in the Lord.
Lord, in your mercy. **Hear our prayer.**

For the spread of the Gospel among those who know nothing of the resurrection

For the sick and dying whom Christ invites in a special way to share in his sufferings so as to share in his resurrection

For the Church, that its faith in the resurrection may be strengthened

Let us pray to Mary, who was filled with joy at her Son's being raised from the dead. **Hail Mary...**

Let us contemplate the risen Christ in silence.

Celebrant Father, it is because of your Son's death and resurrection, and the power of the Holy Spirit, that our prayers are surely heard by you. Guide us today that we may be found worthy to share the resurrection of your Son, who lives and reigns for ever.

2nd SUNDAY OF EASTER

Celebrant We can be sure that we are God's children, so with the trust of children let us open our hearts in prayer for the Church and the world.

Reader Let us pray that the peace Christ promised his followers may be found in our parish and throughout the world.
Lord, hear us. **Lord, graciously hear us.**

Let us pray that like the early Christians, God's people today may be united in heart and soul, and may learn to share their gifts and talents with each other.
Lord, hear us. **Lord, graciously hear us.**

For those who are under strain because of poverty or sickness

For young people and their parents

For those who are prejudiced against immigrants

None of Mary's friends could ever be in want, so let us ask her for friendship and help. **Hail Mary...**

In silence let us pray for our personal desires.

Celebrant Lord God, our Father, we your people come to you with trust that you will hear our prayers, which we make in the name of Jesus, your Son and our Lord.

3rd SUNDAY OF EASTER

Celebrant Like the apostles, the Church today is called on to bear witness to our risen Lord through lives characterised by peace and joy. Through him we are able to come to the Father. Let us do so once again as we make our prayers of petition on behalf of mankind.

Reader We ask that the Church's faith in Jesus as Lord may be fruitful in the love, the joy and the peace of his Spirit.
Lord, in your mercy. **Hear our prayer.**

We pray that Christians may always recognise Jesus in the breaking of bread and in those whom he called the least of his brethren.
Lord, in your mercy. **Hear our prayer.**

For those looking for forgiveness

For the families of those killed in road accidents

For those who are getting married shortly

Mary rejoiced in the Lord. Let us rejoice with her as we say. **Hail Mary...**

In the stillness of our own hearts let us now pray to God.

Celebrant Father, yours is a peace which the world cannot give. Help us to hold fast to it by

4th SUNDAY OF EASTER

Celebrant Jesus presents himself to us as the good shepherd who lays down his life for his sheep. Let us pray that his flock today will show the fidelity and courage needed to follow his lead.

Reader May all men and women, whom Jesus knows and calls each by name, be enabled, through prayer, to lead a life of close friendship with him.
Lord in your mercy. **Hear our prayer.**

May those in trouble call upon him and experience his healing touch, and may all men and women share in his restoring power.
Lord in your mercy. **Hear our prayer.**

For those in authority, that they may learn to see Jesus in others

For the Church, guided by Jesus the Good Shepherd

For those who have died this week

May Mary, who was the first to call on the name of Jesus, offer him our prayers. **Hail Mary...**

Let us pray to Jesus in our hearts.

Celebrant Father, listen to our prayers made in the name of Jesus, the only name by which we can be saved. Bless all your people, including those who are present here, who have come to share the communion of his body and blood, that they may live for ever.

5th SUNDAY OF EASTER

Celebrant We are branches of the true vine, and Jesus invites us to be his disciples. Let us pray that we may bear rich fruit.

Reader May all those who acknowledge Jesus as Son of God be filled with his Spirit so that they may love one another as he commanded.
In your mercy, Lord. **Hear our prayer.**

May the love of the Church for the world be real and active, so that its members may be true bearers of the fruit of the vine.
In your mercy, Lord. **Hear our prayer.**

That neighbours may be kind and open to each other

That Christians may recognise the work of the Spirit among all men

That farmers may enjoy a fruitful season

Let us ask Mary to pray that we too may bring forth the love and truth that were in her. **Hail Mary...**

Let us silently think of our union with Christ and, through him, with all men.

Celebrant Lord God our Father, you are the vinedresser. Prune us but do not cast us away, and we shall bear much fruit, through Christ our Lord.

6th SUNDAY OF EASTER

Celebrant God asks us to love one another. We cannot say we love God if we harm our neighbour. Let us now pray that God's people's love for him may be more than mere words, and may affect the way they live.

Reader We pray for all Christians, that by the example they give, they may help others to come to know God our Father and Jesus Christ whom he has sent.
Lord, hear us. **Lord, graciously hear us.**

Let us pray for all those who show love and care for others, that their example may bear fruit.
Lord, hear us. **Lord, graciously hear us.**

For handicapped people and those who care for them

For those who find it hard to forgive

For those who by quarrelling or through death have lost friends and who are now lonely

We ask Mary, who loved to the uttermost, to share her prayers with ours. **Hail Mary...**

Let us now pray in silence ask God to hear the prayers of our hearts.

Celebrant God the Father, your Son Jesus prayed that we might go out and bear fruit. We know that without your help this is not possible. We now ask your help so that we may live as true followers of Jesus Christ our Lord.

ASCENSION DAY

Celebrant We believe that Jesus is the Lord and Master of all things. In his name we pray to the Father for the Church and all mankind, saying: Lord, hear our prayer.

Reader That the Church will gladly divest itself of anything that obscures its risen and ascended Lord.
We pray to the Father. **Lord, hear our prayer.**

For those who daily pass the doors of our church, that this building will be a sign to them of things they cannot see.
We pray to the Father. **Lord, hear our prayer.**

For those unable to worship because of illness

For those who know they are dying

For those from whom the truth has been hidden

We pray to God in union with our Lady, saying.
Hail Mary...

Let us now stand before God in a few moments of silence.

Celebrant Lord God, you are above all, and over all. May we never doubt your power; may we never doubt your love; you who live and reign for ever and ever.

7th SUNDAY OF EASTER

Celebrant Eastertide is a time for renewal, for hope and for joy in Christ's message. On this last day of the Easter season let us pray for all things to be made new.

Reader Let us pray for all those who have recently been baptised. May the new life they have received enable them to face the future with hope and confidence.
Lord, in your mercy. **Hear our prayer.**

Let us pray for those who have been confirmed. May the strength of the Spirit be with them and keep them true in times of trial.
Lord, in your mercy . **Hear our prayer.**

For those whose marriage seems to be failing

For those in need of the sacrament of reconciliation

For the sick and the dying

Let us ask our Lady, the Mother of the Church, to add her prayers to ours. **Hail Mary...**

Let us pray in silence for our own intentions.

Celebrant God our Father, we pray that we may be the instruments of your love in the world. May we receive in full what we ask for in faith. We make our prayer through Christ our Lord.

PENTECOST SUNDAY

Celebrant The Spirit of God came to the apostles so that they could speak to the world about the wonderful works of God. Let us pray for that Spirit to be with God's people as they are sent out into the world.

Reader Let us pray for the Church, that all the gifts of the Spirit may work in its members, and that they may recognize the different gifts in one another.
Come Holy Spirit. **Fill the hearts of your faithful.**

Let us pray for all men and women, that the love, patience, kindness and gentleness of the Spirit may rule their hearts and deeds.
Come Holy Spirit. **Fill the hearts of your faithful.**

For those who are not at peace with themselves or their fellow men

For those who have quarrelled with partner, parent, child or friend

For non-Christians who are searching for God's Spirit

Let us pray that like Mary all may be obedient to the Spirit. **Hail Mary...**

God's Spirit is in our hearts; let us be still and know him.

Celebrant Lord God, you have shown yourself in the power and warmth of your Spirit. Send your Spirit so that all may walk with confidence and humility. We make our prayer through Christ our Lord.

CORPUS CHRISTI

Celebrant God has promised that he will be with us always. The Eucharist is the sign of that promise, the new covenant. Let us pray that all God's people may recognise and respond to his promise.

Reader We pray that all men and women will come to know Christ in his followers by the sign of breaking of bread and the fact of sharing of life.
Bread of life. **Hear our prayer.**

We pray that the Church will share the spirit of Christ's sacrifice as it shares his body and blood, and be an instrument of service to the world.
Bread of life. **Hear our prayer.**

For those who worship false gods, that they may discover the truth

For those who live for themselves, that they may come to know God in others

For those who have often been let down, that they may know that God's promise always stands

Let us ask Mary, who pondered God's mysteries in her heart, to pray with us. **Hail Mary...**

Let us pray in silence for the needs of the world.

Celebrant Lord God, you have given us your Son that we might have life. We pray that we may always treasure this gift and share it with others, for ever and ever.

TRINITY SUNDAY

Celebrant Today we worship God as three-in-one: Father, Son and Holy Spirit. So we make our prayers to the Father through the Son for all his people whom he gathers together in his Spirit.

Reader Let us pray for all those who have received the gift of baptism, that they may follow Christ, on whom the Spirit rested at his baptism.
Lord, in your mercy. **Hear our prayer.**

Let us pray for all those who have received the gifts of the Spirit in great measure. May the use them wisely and to the glory of the Father.
Lord, in your mercy. **Hear our prayer.**

For all our fellow men and women, through whom God's love comes to us

For people in the troubled parts of the world, that the light of the Spirit may shine on them

For the poor and oppressed, that Jesus may be seen in them

May Mary pray with us, that Christ may be formed in our lives. **Hail Mary...**

With the Spirit of Jesus in us, let us pray in the silence of our hearts.

Celebrant God our Father, we come to you with our prayers as your children, with your Son Jesus Christ, whose Spirit teaches us. Hear our prayers through him who lives and reigns with you and the Spirit for ever and ever.

THE SACRED HEART

Celebrant Let us look on the pierced side of Jesus on the cross and ask that this love that gave everything may fill the world.

Reader Let us pray that Jesus, through his everlasting love, may make his Church strong in faith and love to serve him and all mankind.
Let us pray to the Lord. **Lord, hear our prayer.**

Let us pray that those who believe in the Father may remain strong in their belief through the Son who poured out his love for them.
Let us pray to the Lord. **Lord, hear our prayer.**

That those who have not experienced the love of family or of friends may do so

That those sunk in hate, dislike and lovelessness may shake them off

That those who cannot trust other people may do so through God's love

Let us ask Mary to teach us the certainty of her love for Christ. **Hail Mary...**

Let us think in silence of the great mystery of Jesus's love.

Celebrant God our Father, you loved the world so much that you sent your Son, who poured out his blood that the world might be saved. Hear the prayers we make to you in his name, that his love in us may never fail.

1st SUNDAY IN ORDINARY TIME

The Baptism of Our Lord

Celebrant Jesus is Lord of all. Since he became one of us, we can join our prayers to the Father with his as we pray for the world he came to save.

Reader Let us pray for all God's people, that they may live as his sons and daughters, knowing that they are loved by him and pleasing to him.
Hear us, O Lord. **And answer our prayer.**

Let us pray for all those who are afraid of God, who dare not listen to his voice in prayer, that they may come to accept the Gospel in the depth of their hearts.
Hear us, O Lord. **And answer our prayer.**

For those who work in all the media of communications

For trade union leaders and employers

For the sick and those who care for them

Mary accepted God's invitation to bring Jesus into the world. We ask her to pray for us. **Hail Mary...**

Let us offer the Father quiet prayer, knowing his universal love.

Celebrant Father, baptism and membership of your family is a gift we have received from others. Help your people to be serious in their faith and to be ready to share it with others. We make our prayer through Christ our Lord.

2nd SUNDAY IN ORDINARY TIME

Celebrant Isaiah speaks of God's love for his people as that of a bridegroom for his bride. Let us, in the knowledge of his constant love, pray for the faithless world.

Reader Let us pray for all sinners, that they may turn back to God and so enjoy his constant love.
We pray to the Lord. **Lord, hear our prayer.**

Let us pray for the Church, the bride of Christ, that with the help of the Holy Spirit its members may be ever faithful to their vows.
We pray to the Lord. **Lord, hear our prayer.**

For married people, that they may have forgiveness and understanding

For the clergy, that they may value the gifts of their flock

For all who have chosen not to marry, that their love may not be turned in on themselves but go out to others

When the wine ran out at the marriage feast Mary was eager to help. Let us ask her prayers for those for whom we pray. **Hail Mary...**

God has called us to the wedding feast. Let us pray in silence that all may be found worthy to be present.

Celebrant God our Father, we pray that the world may be full of hope even in times of trouble, knowing that its future is in your hands. We make our prayer through Christ our Lord.

3rd SUNDAY IN ORDINARY TIME

Celebrant All God's people are members of one family, of which Jesus is the head. Let us pray that all may give what they can and receive what they need, and so build up Christ's Church.

Reader We pray for all communities that share the eucharistic meal. May their sharing at the altar spill over into service of others.
Lord, hear us. **Lord, graciously hear us.**

We pray for all those who preach or teach the word of God, that the Spirit may be with them and help them to proclaim the good news.
Lord, hear us. **Lord, graciously hear us.**

For members of other Christian Churches and bodies

For the lonely and depressed

For the teachers in our schools and parishes

Let us put our prayers in the hands of Mary, mother of Jesus and of the Church. **Hail Mary...**

Let us pray silently for our own needs.

Celebrant Father, you ask all to use the gifts you have given them for the good of your family. Hear our prayers that the Church may give Jesus to the world. We make our prayer in his name, Jesus the Lord.

4th SUNDAY IN ORDINARY TIME

Celebrant Love is a gift from God. We express our love by asking for an increase of this gift for all who are in need.

Reader Let us pray for all those whose love is weak and unsure, that in the Spirit they may come to have patience, kindness and forgiveness.
Christ our life. **Hear and answer our prayer.**

Let us pray for all those who work overseas, that their sacrifice of home and country may be rewarded with a rich harvest.
Christ our life. **Hear and answer our prayer.**

For those who work for greater justice and tolerance in the world

For priests, sisters, teachers and other parish workers

For those who work for international relief agencies

The first to learn from the personal love of Jesus was his mother. Let us ask her to pray for us in our need to learn. **Hail Mary...**

Let us pray for a moment in silence.

Celebrant Our Father, you sent your Son to show the way to you through love of our fellow men and women. As we make our prayers to you through him, may we come to the kingdom where he dwells with you and the Spirit for ever.

5th SUNDAY IN ORDINARY TIME

Celebrant Jesus commissions his people to spread the word of God to the ends of the earth. We pray that they may have the strength to fulfil this task faithfully and with perseverance.

Reader For the Church, that it may help all men and women know that Jesus is Saviour, and that he invites them to discover eternal life with their Father in heaven, we pray to the Lord.
Lord, hear our prayer. **Lord, hear our prayer.**

For governments and all in positions of authority, that they may help bring peace in their own countries and may join together to create a world of equality and justice, we pray to the Lord.
Lord, hear our prayer. **Lord, hear our prayer.**

For journalists and all who earn their living by the use of words, that truth may prevail

That many may respond to the call of Jesus and give their lives to preaching his word

For the deaf, that their needs may be met with due understanding

Mary teaches us by her example of faithfulness and self-giving. We seek the help of her prayers as we say together. **Hail Mary...**

Let us pray in the silence of our hearts that free from fear all may come to the knowledge of Jesus.

Celebrant Heavenly Father, strengthen your Church and help it to be a living example of the presence of your word in the world. Accept our efforts to be faithful to the message of your Son, who lives with you for ever.

6th SUNDAY IN ORDINARY TIME

Celebrant Let us remember that Christ has been raised from the dead, and call to him with confidence.

Reader May Christ lead all who know poverty and hunger, sadness and rejection, yet to find happiness.
We pray to you, Lord. **Lord, hear our prayer.**

May the poor, hungry and sorrowful who have trusted in God and looked for his aid, find an answer to their prayer.
We pray to you, Lord. **Lord, hear our prayer.**

For those who do not know Christ

For those who have no friends

For those who suffer because they are Christians

Let us ask Mary, who was poor and humble of heart, to keep our minds and hearts like hers. **Hail Mary...**

In silence, let us feel the real poverty of the world, and its need for God's help.

Celebrant Heavenly Father, you sent your Son to show us your kingdom here on earth. May he guide us in your ways so that we may come through him to know you in the Spirit.

7th SUNDAY IN ORDINARY TIME

Celebrant God is our compassionate Father who knows and loves each of us by name. With his Son at our side, let us put our prayers before him.

Reader Let us pray for a spirit of generosity in the Church, that its members may think generously of others, remembering that if they judge not, they will not be judged.
In your mercy, Lord. **Hear our prayer.**

Let us pray for a spirit of kindness and compassion in the world, particularly among those in authority, that they may not condemn others for their weakness and failures.
In your mercy, Lord. **Hear our prayer.**

For ungrateful people, that they may learn to count their blessings

For those rich in the world's goods, that they may find real happiness

For those who are downtrodden by circumstances, that they may be raised to new hope

Let us ask Mary and all the saints to join their prayers with ours. **Hail Mary...**

In silence let us call on God for his gifts of mercy and compassion.

Celebrant O God and Father of all mankind, may your Spirit give your people the strength to love as you do, to love without expecting any return. We ask this in the name of Jesus Christ, who loved without end, and now lives for ever.

8th SUNDAY IN ORDINARY TIME

Celebrant The word of God speaks of life, of truth, of goodness. Let us pray that these may spread through this disordered and uncertain world.

Reader Let us pray for the whole Church; that it may speak the word of God more effectively in its teaching and in its life.
Lord, hear our prayer. **Lord, hear our prayer.**

Let us pray for those who spread the word in their working lives. May the example they show win over men's hearts and minds.
Lord, hear our prayer. **Lord, hear our prayer.**

For those whose business is words

For those near death

For the faithful and the unfaithful departed

Mary always kept God's word in her heart. Let us ask for her prayers. **Hail Mary...**

Let us pray for a moment in silence.

Celebrant Father, your Son Jesus was the conqueror of death. Grant that risen, he may live always in our hearts and be the source of our speech and action. We make our prayer through the same Jesus Christ our Lord.

9th SUNDAY IN ORDINARY TIME

Celebrant The centurion placed his trust completely in Jesus. Let us now pray with equal confidence to the Father through Christ.

Reader We pray that the Church may read the signs of the times, recognizing the word and truth of the Lord even in unexpected quarters.
Lord, hear us. **Lord, graciously hear us.**

We pray that all men and women will come to know God's universal love, finding their own different ways to knowledge and confidence.
Lord, hear us. **Lord, graciously hear us.**

For the gifts of Christian unity and understanding between people of all faiths

For those concerned with preserving the environment

For those in need

We join our prayers with those of Mary who trusted completely in God. **Hail Mary...**

In silence now let us place ourselves before God, simply and trustingly.

Celebrant Father, we who are your family are weak and our faith often falters. Strengthen your people so that others may know that true strength is found in you. We make our prayer through your Son Jesus Christ.

10th SUNDAY IN ORDINARY TIME

Celebrant As the widow of Nain turned to our Lord for comfort in her distress, so we in our turn pray to him, that he will comfort the world in its distress.

Reader That the sick and the lonely, those who sorrow and mourn, may find help and comfort, we pray to the Lord.
Lord, hear us. **Lord, graciously hear us.**

That Christians may learn the meaning of conversion, turning ever and again to Christ in their hearts when they fail, we pray to the Lord.
Lord, hear us. **Lord graciously hear us.**

For all those who have recently lost someone they love

For those struggling with difficult and uncongenial tasks

For those who have lost their means of livelihood

That Mary's prayers may be added to ours as we pray for all mankind, we pray. **Hail Mary...**

Let us pray silently for a while.

Celebrant Father, you are always forgiving the sin of the world and comforting your people. Be with us now as we turn to you with our prayers, through Christ our Lord.

11th SUNDAY IN ORDINARY TIME

Celebrant Conscious of the sin of the world and of our need for God's help, let us turn to him in prayer.

Reader Let us pray for all Christians, that they may know themselves as God knows them, and be truly sorry for their sins.
Lord, in your mercy. **Hear our prayer.**

Let us pray for the governments of the nations, that they may seek to put the resources of technology at the service of peace and justice, not of war and profit.
Lord, in your mercy. **Hear our prayer.**

For those in need of the sacrament of reconciliation which brings pardon and peace

For those whose work in the entertainment world makes our lives richer and more enjoyable

For the sick who find their suffering difficult to accept

Mary prays to her Son for sinners, and so we say.
Hail Mary...

We pray quietly for forgiveness.

Celebrant Father, your word teaches us that man's repentance is more than matched by your forgivenes. Give us the true spirit of repentance, through Christ our Lord.

12th SUNDAY IN ORDINARY TIME

Celebrant Let us pray to God, the Lord who dwells in our midst, for the people he has won for himself.

Reader Let us pray for the Church, that its leaders and people may be firm in their faith and always willing to confess it before the world.
In your mercy, Lord. **Hear our prayer.**

Let us pray for young people, that they may face up to their growing responsibilities and not run away from them through alcohol and other drugs.
In your mercy, Lord. **Hear our prayer.**

For those who have wide responsibilities entrusted to them

For those who have fallen victim to various forms of evil

For those who face trial

Mary's son was a friend to outcasts and sinners. Let us ask her that we may share in his friendship. **Hail Mary...**

Let us place our thoughts and needs silently in the hands of the good shepherd.

Celebrant Father, we know we have only to ask in order to receive. May our requests be in accordance with your will, as we make them through Christ our Lord.

13th SUNDAY IN ORDINARY TIME

Celebrant If we are led by the Spirit no law can touch us. In that same Spirit we now pray to the Father.

Reader For the Church all over the world, that people will resolutely follow the Lord and build up the kingdom of God, we pray to the Lord.
Lord, hear us. **Lord, graciously hear us.**

For Elizabeth our Queen, for the government of our country, and for those in positions of great political or moral influence, we pray to the Lord.
Lord, hear us. **Lord, graciously hear us.**

For those labelled as misfits or dropouts, and those judged only by their appearances

For those who choose their own way to holiness

For those who cannot see what God has done for them

We ask our Lady, the mother of all God's people to pray with us. **Hail Mary...**

In our own words we speak to God from whom no secret can be hidden.

Celebrant Father, may these our prayers help to show us the kingdom of your Son, through the working of the Spirit in whom we make our prayer to you.

14th SUNDAY IN ORDINARY TIME

Celebrant God consoles and enriches his people with new life. Let us pray that the Church may receive that life in abundance and pass it on to the world.

Reader That men and women throughout the world may come to eternal life through meeting followers of Christ and hearing the Gospel, we pray to the Lord.
Lord, hear our prayer. **Lord, hear our prayer.**

That the good news of the Gospel may be a source of peace to those who preach it and to those who hear it, we pray to the Lord.
Lord, hear our prayer. **Lord, hear our prayer.**

For those shaken and discouraged by the wickedness around them

For those whose lives are deprived and spoiled by the violence, greed or heartless neglect of others

For those who find it hard to feel enthusiasm in their work for the Church

Let us ask Mary, who brought the new life into the world, to join her prayers to ours, as we say. **Hail Mary...**

Let us pray in silence that our wishes may be in accordance with God's will.

Celebrant Father, you are closer to your people than they know. Give us the grace to recognize your life in ourselves and in all the others for whom we pray through Christ, Your Son, our Lord.

15th SUNDAY IN ORDINARY TIME

Celebrant Today's gospel tells us that anyone who needs help is our neighbour. We know that we cannot come to the Father except through the Son, whom we meet in our neighbour, so let us pray for all those in need of help.

Reader We pray that all Christians will play their part in setting aside envy and dissension in the world, so that those in need will have their wants fulfilled.
Lord, in your mercy. **Hear our prayer.**

We pray that the pilgrim Church in the world may make disciples of all nations and show their leaders that God's authority is not power but service.
Lord, in your mercy. **Hear our prayer.**

For spastic and disabled children

For workers in relief agencies

For doctors and nurses

We ask Mary, our mother, to pray with us.
Hail Mary...

In a moment of silent prayer, let us think of all those in need.

Celebrant Father, we know that no one can love you whom he cannot see unless he loves his neighbour whom he can see. Teach us to see your Son in those who suffer like him, through whom we make our prayer to you.

16th SUNDAY IN ORDINARY TIME

Celebrant God reveals himself to men of faith in every age. Let us pray that the faith of Abraham may inspire God's people today.

Reader We pray for all those who lead a busy life. May they find time to listen to the word of God.
In your mercy, Lord. **Hear our prayer.**

We pray for all those who are suffering. May they find strength and comfort in Christ, who suffered for the sin of the world.
In your mercy, Lord. **Hear our prayer.**

For those who have lost someone they love

For those who are frightened of bearing a child

For those who use the roads

Let us ask Mary to join with us in prayer. **Hail Mary...**

In silence let us listen to the Lord as he speaks to us.

Celebrant Lord God our Father, you are with your people at all times. Strengthen our faith, help us to understand your word to us, and hear the prayers we make to you through Christ your Son.

17th SUNDAY IN ORDINARY TIME

Celebrant Christ our Saviour urges us to approach God with trust and confidence since he is our Father and we are his children. Let us do so, remembering that Jesus himself says, 'Ask the Father anything in my name.'

Reader Let us pray for our fellow-Christians, offering up their prayers in faith. May their wishes be in accordance with God's will.
Lord, hear us. **Lord, in your mercy hear us.**

Let us pray for the Church in our own diocese. May it be a powerhouse of love and prayer in the community.
Lord, hear us. **Lord, in your mercy hear us.**

For those who have received special gifts from God

For those who are soon to be confirmed

For those who have just moved into the parish

It was at the request of Mary his mother that Jesus worked his first great sign at Cana. Let us now pray with her.
Hail Mary...

Reassured by the words of the Gospel, let us now pray quietly for our individual intentions.

Celebrant Almighty Lord and gracious Father, we know that you are the giver of all good. Listen to our prayers of petition and grant that all our lawful desires may find fulfilment through the same Christ our Lord.

18th SUNDAY IN ORDINARY TIME

Celebrant Whatever we do we are always unprofitable servants. We are not self-sufficient and we bring our needs and those of all mankind to God.

Reader We pray that Christians will have the courage to seek the things that last, not set their hearts on what is perishable.
Lord, in your mercy. **Hear our prayer.**

We pray that the rich nations of the world will learn to conserve and share the world's resources, not flaunt their greed in front of the poor.
Lord, in your mercy. **Hear our prayer.**

That politicians may guide the country on a course based on the Gospel

That our local community will always show a spirit of openness and welcome to outsiders

That those who are dying will know how to meet Christ without their riches and property

May Mary pray that we will learn from her Son what it means to be poor and humble. **Hail Mary...**

Let us ask the Father to speak to us in our hearts.

Celebrant Father, the world is full of false gods. Strip away the idolatry of our hearts. May your people love others as you love them. We make our prayer through Christ our Lord.

19th SUNDAY IN ORDINARY TIME

Celebrant The God of Abraham, Isaac and Jacob, who brought his People out of Egypt, has made his covenant with us. Let us pray that his people's response will not fail.

Reader We pray for the Church, that it may be always wholly committed to God's service and alert to the signs of his coming.
Lord, save your people. **Lord, save your people.**

We pray for all who find life difficult, that they may cease to feel world-weary and learn to trust in the Lord.
Lord, save your people. **Lord, save your people.**

For those who especially need patience: the incurably ill, parents of handicapped children

For those crippled by fear, loneliness, frustration and lack of purpose

For those who have special responsibilities in our local community

Mary believed that God would fulfil his promise. We ask her to pray with us. **Hail Mary...**

In silence let us commend ourselves and all for whom we have prayed into God's fatherly hands.

Celebrant Loving Father, hear our prayers. Though your answer may seem to be delayed, give us the faith to trust your promise, through Jesus Christ our Lord.

20th SUNDAY IN ORDINARY TIME

Celebrant The readings remind us that Christian life demands courage and resolution. Let us pray that God's people may keep their eyes on Jesus, who sustains their faith and brings it to perfection.

Reader We pray that the power of the Spirit may enable the Church to triumph over evil and persevere in following Jesus.
Lord, in your mercy. **Hear our prayer.**

We pray that human rights and human freedom may be respected, particularly by those who call themselves Christians.
Lord, in your mercy. **Hear our prayer.**

That nations may seek a peaceful solution to their problems

That the world's resources may be shared

That those who work to relieve suffering may find support

Let us pray to Mary who consented to suffer with her Son, that his work might be brought to completion.
Hail Mary...

Let us pray in silence for the help we need.

Celebrant Help us, Father, to rely on you in the struggle against evil in the world. Let us remember that Jesus is with us and will give us all the help we need. We make our prayer in his name, Jesus the Lord.

21st SUNDAY IN ORDINARY TIME

Celebrant Today we can be particularly aware of the universality of the Church, so let us pray for the needs of peoples of different creeds, colour and culture.

Reader Let us pray for people in all their variety, that all may be able to play their part freely in building up God's kingdom of justice and peace.
Lord, hear us. **Lord, graciously hear us.**

Let us pray for the Churches of the Third World, that their struggle against oppression may lead to real growth in freedom.
Lord, hear us. **Lord, graciously hear us.**

For the Jewish people, those in Israel, those scattered among every nation

For those who are suffering, that with God's help they may be able to bear their pain

For those who are near to despair, or tempted to suicide

Let us ask Mary, the mother of the universal Church, to pray for us. **Hail Mary...**

Let us make God present to us in the intimacy of silence.

Celebrant Help us, Father, to work for goodness and righteousness throughout the world, and to be free of prejudice. We ask this in the name of Jesus the Lord.

22nd SUNDAY IN ORDINARY TIME

Celebrant The way of the world is not the way of Jesus. Let us pray that his way of gentleness and humility will be our way.

Reader We pray for the poor, the sick and the lonely, that they may find in Christians ready agents of care and compassion.
Lord, hear us. **Lord, in your mercy hear us.**

We pray for Christians everywhere, that they may stand ever in the Lord's presence and take him as their model of conduct in all situations.
Lord, hear us. **Lord, in your mercy hear us.**

For those who are in positions of authority

For the Pope and the bishops, that they may provide us with authentic leadership

For those involved in parish concerns

Mary in her humility is a symbol of the whole Church. We ask her to pray for the salvation of all. **Hail Mary...**

Let us now pray in humility and silence

Celebrant Heavenly Father, hear your people's prayers and keep us close to your Son, who is the way, the truth and the life, for ever and ever.

23rd SUNDAY IN ORDINARY TIME

Celebrant We are told that those who seek the highest place will be humbled. Let us pray that men and women will learn to recognize their true dignity as children of God.

Reader For those who close their eyes to the difficulties of their neighbours, that their eyes may be opened, we pray to the Lord.
In your mercy, Lord. **Hear our prayer.**

For those who work in organizations for the care of the poor and the sick, that they may find strength to continue their work, we pray to the Lord.
In your mercy, Lord. **Hear our prayer.**

For those who are too busy to see where needs lie

For those who turn their backs on conditions in the Third World

For those who fail to grasp opportunities to help

Mary stood at the foot of the cross sharing the suffering of her Son. May we gain strength from her example as we say. **Hail Mary...**

We now pause and pray in a spirit of humility.

Celebrant Heavenly Father, help us to know ourselves as we truly are, utterly dependent on you for all we have. As we prepare to bring our gifts to the altar, bring us to make a gift of our lives in service to others, like your Son, Christ our Lord.

24th SUNDAY IN ORDINARY TIME

Celebrant Our God is a shepherd who goes in search of the lost sheep, who longs for the sinner to repent. Let us pray that all those who have strayed may find their way back.

Reader Let us pray for those who are cut off from the Church. May they find Christ's love and welcome when they return.
Lord, hear us. **Lord, graciously hear us.**

Let us pray for those who persecute the Church of Christ. Like Saul, may they learn the error of their ways and become apostles of Christ.
Lord, hear us. **Lord, graciously hear us.**

For men of violence, and for their victims

For those who cheat their fellow men

For those who misuse the gifts God has given them

Let us commend our prayers to Mary, who prays for sinners now and always. **Hail Mary...**

Let us reach out in silence to God on behalf of all those we pray for.

Celebrant God our Father, whose pardon is always waiting for those who seek it, we ask you to hear our prayers on behalf of all who have sinned, through Christ our Lord.

25th SUNDAY IN ORDINARY TIME

Celebrant God our Father sent his Son that all might be saved. Let us pray for all our brothers and sisters.

Reader We pray for all who are in positions of authority in our land, and ask that they may be given wisdom.
Lord, hear us. **Lord, graciously hear us.**

We pray for all who hold ministries in the Church and ask that they may fulfil their obligations with joy and peace.
Lord, hear us. **Lord, graciously hear us.**

For employers and employees, that they may deal justly and honestly with each other

For those who are on holiday, and those about to retire

For those prevented from working by illness, that they may experience the encouragement and support of their fellow men

Let us ask Mary to pray with us. **Hail Mary...**

We will now pause to ask God to help all work conscientiously.

Celebrant Father, we are surrounded by the works of your hands; we pray that they may be put to good use, through Christ our Lord.

26th SUNDAY IN ORDINARY TIME

Celebrant God's word reminds us that the first in the kingdom are the poor and helpless. Let us pray for them and for all mankind.

Reader Let us pray for those whose lives are a failure in human terms, that Christ's apparent human failure may be seen reflected in them.
Lord, hear us. **And grant our prayer.**

Let us pray for those whose lives are secure, that they may not be self-satisfied, and for the rich, that they may not be lost.
Lord, hear us. **And grant our prayer.**

For those who are near despair

For a spirit of poverty in the Church

For the poor and oppressed of the Third World

Mary in her poverty was an agent of God's riches. May she pray with us as we say. **Hail Mary...**

In a moment's silence let us ponder the needs of those we pray for.

Celebrant Father, you have promised us the blessing of your kingdom. Grant us the poverty of spirit that will make us merit these blessings, through Jesus Christ our Lord.

27th SUNDAY IN ORDINARY TIME

Celebrant Let us now turn to the God and Father of Jesus Christ and make our prayers to him with faith and trust.

Reader We pray that the Church may persevere in prayer and action and not lose faith and trust in God, even if at times it cannot hear his voice.

Lord, hear our prayer. **And let our cry come to you.**

We pray that Christians may acknowledge their complete dependence on God, and willingly turn to him for their needs.

Lord, hear our prayer. **And let our cry come to you.**

For those who are forced to earn their living in immoral ways

For politicians who may find it difficult to be truthful

For those who have to work away from their families and homes

Let us pray with Mary who trusted so willingly in God. **Hail Mary...**

Let us pray quietly for a moment.

Celebrant Father, your reply when we turn to you is a still, small voice. May we not lose faith and trust but learn to recognize your voice, following the example of your own Son, who lives and reigns with you for ever.

28th SUNDAY IN ORDINARY TIME

Celebrant We often turn to God and forget his continued goodness to us. In our Prayers now let us ask for his gifts to be known and understood.

Reader We pray for those who know the joys of helath, happiness and security; may they always be conscious of their dependence on God's love.
Lord, we pray. **Hear our prayer.**

We pray for those who have faith; may they continue to hope in God's goodness and never be tempted to complacency.
Lord, we pray. **Hear our prayer.**

For those who work for greater unity among the Churches in this area

For those who heal others by their words and skill

For those who make the world a safer place to live in

Our Lady thanked God for his goodness to her; she glorified the Lord and her spirit rejoiced in God her saviour. We now join with her in prayer. **Hail Mary...**

Let us pray in silence for all who have received special gifts.

Celebrant Father, you give to all your gifts in due season. May your people learn to make good use of them, and so come to know you in the happiness of your kingdom, with Christ our Lord.

29th SUNDAY IN ORDINARY TIME

Celebrant Today's lesson is one of promise and of hope. We must pray continually and never lose heart. Let us pray to the Lord.

Reader That the Church will have confidence that the gates of hell will not prevail against it, and work steadfastly for the eradication of evil in the world, we pray to the Lord.
Lord, hear our prayer. **And let our cry come to you.**

That we Christians may work for justice for the oppressed, through love of God and respect for our fellow men, we pray to the Lord.
Lord, hear our prayer. **And let our cry come to you.**

For those who do not realize that forgiveness is always waiting for them

For a spirit of cooperation among Christian churches in the area, that God's work may be accomplished

For all who contribute to the celebration of Mass, that they may find happiness in such service to the community

That our Lady's prayers may inspire us to unselfish service to others, we pray. **Hail Mary...**

Let us now pray in silence for our own intentions.

Celebrant Lord, may your love ever direct men's hearts, for without your grace we are nothing. We make our prayer through Christ our Lord.

30th SUNDAY IN ORDINARY TIME

Celebrant When Jesus says, 'blessed are the poor in spirit', he is praising those who put no trust in their own resources. Aware that we have nothing that is not given by the Father, let us now pray to him in Jesus' name.

Reader We pray that all God's people will learn true humility, which results in action, not the false humility which is often an excuse for inaction.
Lord, hear us. **And grant our prayer.**

We pray that those in authority will see an example of strength in the humility of Christ, not in power as the world knows it.
Lord, hear us. **And grant our prayer.**

For those who are unsure of themselves and who have opted out of society

For those who have to rely on others for their basic needs

For those who work on land or sea to provide others with food

Because of her humility Mary was raised up by God her saviour. Encouraged by her example let us now say.
Hail Mary...

For a few moments let us stand in humility and silence before God.

Celebrant God our Father, through the life, death and resurrection of your Son, you have shown what humility is. Help your people to follow him in all things and so seek the glory that he was raised to. We make our prayer in his name, Jesus the Lord.

31st SUNDAY IN ORDINARY TIME

Celebrant The Lord is good to all and compassionate to all his creatures; that is why we can be sure he will listen to our prayers.

Reader Let us pray for all who have led a materialistic life; may they, like Zacchaeus, be converted and share in Christ's new life.
Lord, hear us. **Lord, graciously hear us.**

Let us pray for all those living in countries where the Gospel has not yet been preached; may they in their own way find Christ and have eternal life with him.
Lord, hear us. **Lord, graciously hear us.**

For the eradication of religious bigotry in our communities

For the royal family

For those who have died in the past week

Let us call on Mary's motherly care. **Hail Mary...**

Let us pray for a moment in silence.

Celebrant Lord God, implant in the hearts of your people the desire to know and love you above all things. Let them not count the cost but place all their trust in you. We make our prayer through Christ our Lord.

32nd SUNDAY IN ORDINARY TIME

Celebrant Let us turn in prayer to God who is rich in mercy to all who call upon him. Let us pray for the Church and all the needy.

Reader Let us pray that the Church may show real faith in the resurrection of Jesus and so lead all men and women from the death of sin to a new life in Christ.
Lord, in your mercy. **Hear our prayer.**

Let us pray that the Pope and the bishops may be nourished in their mission by the prayers and support of the faithful.
Lord, in your mercy. **Hear our prayer.**

That those who have died will enjoy the fellowship of the saints

That those who suffer persecution will be rescued

That those engaged in strife will turn to peaceful means

Let us ask Mary to pray for us now and at the hour of our death. **Hail Mary...**

Let us put before God our various needs.

Celebrant Father, you are our strength in time of need. Listen to our prayers and lead us to your kingdom, through Christ our Lord.

33rd SUNDAY IN ORDINARY TIME

Celebrant Christ has called us together. He is here in our midst. In his name let us pray to the Father.

Reader We pray that all who hold office in the Church will follow the humble example of Jesus, so that their endurance will win them eternal life.
Lord, hear us. **Lord, graciously hear us.**

We pray for all those tempted, in a world of violence, to disbelieve in the love of God, or in the goodness of their fellow men, that they may find faith.
Lord, hear us. **Lord, graciously hear us.**

For those whose consciences are disturbed because they are involved in the manufacture of weapons of war

For those trying to begin again after failure or disappointment

For those who for whatever reason feel unable to receive Holy Communion

With the whole Church we honour our Lady, who bore for us the word of God. **Hail Mary...**

We may not find the words with which to pray, but we offer God the silence of our hearts.

Celebrant God our Father, your Son came into the world to give mankind the message of eternal life. May his Spirit take root in our hearts and inspire our actions. We ask this through Christ our Lord, your Son.

34th SUNDAY IN ORDINARY TIME

Christ the King

Celebrant As we come to the close of the Church's year, let us consider the meaning of the kingship of Christ as shown in his life, and pray that all mankind may come to his kingdom.

Reader Let us pray that Christians will help the blind to see, the lame to walk and the poor to hear the good news, and so work to build up Christ's kingdom.
Lord, in your mercy. **Hear our prayer.**

Let us pray for those who hold positions of authority in the world, that they may see the kingship of Christ as a call to service.
Lord, in your mercy. **Hear our prayer.**

For those who are searching for forgiveness

For those who suffer sickness, loneliness or want

For justice, harmony, and peace in our society

Let us turn to Mary, who by the grace of Christ was without sin, and ask her to pray now for us sinners. **Hail Mary...**

May the light and peace of Christ be with us as we pray in silence.

Celebrant Father, so change your people by your healing love, that they all may hear your Son say: You will be with me in paradise. We make our prayer in his name, Jesus our King for ever.

1st SUNDAY OF ADVENT

Celebrant God reveals himself in Jesus to those who look and wait for him. Let us pray that during this season of Advent his people will prepare for the coming festival of Christmas by prayerful faith.

Reader We pray that Christian communities throughout the world will listen attentively to God's word, and so be prepared to receive him with an increased faith.
We pray to the Lord. **Lord, hear our prayer.**

We pray that the world will hear the Christian message and that Christians will play a leading part in working for peace.
We pray to the Lord. **Lord, hear our prayer.**

For those who feel they need to change direction

For those who find it hard to listen

For those who cannot pray

Let us make our prayer with Mary, who waited for the coming of Jesus with joy and love. **Hail Mary...**

Let us pray silently.

Celebrant God our Father, increase the faith, hope and love of your people as they await the coming of your Son, Jesus the Lord.

2nd SUNDAY OF ADVENT

Celebrant God calls us to rejoice at the coming of our Saviour. Let us make ready to greet him with love, by praying for the needs of his people.

Reader Let us pray that the Gospel may be spread to all parts of the world, so that peoples everywhere may share in the joy of Christ's coming.
We pray to the Lord. **Lord, hear our prayer.**

Let us pray that God's prophets and messengers in the world may be recognised and listened to.
We pray to the Lord. **Lord, hear our prayer.**

That missionaries may love those they are sent to

That every Christian may be an evangelist

That the joy of the gospel message be not lost in controversy and criticism

Let us ask Mary to pray with us that we may share her glad expectation of Christ's coming. **Hail Mary...**

In silence, away from the noise of the world, let us dedicate ourselves to God's service.

Celebrant God our Father, you sent your prophets and messengers of old to prepare a straight way for the coming of your Son. May we and all Christians be those prophets and messengers today as we wait in joyful hope for the coming of our Lord.

3rd SUNDAY OF ADVENT

Celebrant The Mass today is one of joy because we know that Christ is coming. Let us now share this joy of Christ being with us by praying for the needs of the world.

Reader Let us pray for all those members of the Church who feel cut off from Christ's love. May they come to share in his life and follow him.

Lord, hear us. **Lord, graciously hear us.**

Let us pray for those who guide the affairs of the world. May they seek example and encouragement in Christ's word.

Lord, hear us. **Lord, graciously hear us.**

For the Church, that it may be a true source of guidance

For all who need a good example

For those who need to find Christ close at hand

Our Lady was deeply grateful to God for the gift of her Son. May we share her joy as we say. **Hail Mary...**

Let us now in silence pray for all those who wait and hope.

Celebrant Father, we your people are often unfaithful to you and yet you always love us. We pray that we may learn to appreciate and be grateful for all your gifts. We make our prayer through Christ our Lord.

4th SUNDAY OF ADVENT

Celebrant Let us pray to the Father, who sends us his Son, Jesus Christ, and let us pray for all his people.

Reader We pray for those lacking in human dignity and respect. May this coming Christmas bring them recognition as children of God.
Let us pray to the Lord. **Lord, hear our prayer.**

We pray for those of other faiths. May the way in which they receive God in their lives bring them peace and comfort.
Let us pray to the Lord. **Lord, hear our prayer.**

For all those who carry a heavy burden of responsibility

For travellers, that they may have a safe journey and a happy homecoming

For all those in need of help in our community

Let us pray to Mary who received the Word of God in confidence and faith. **Hail Mary...**

Our Lord told us to come to him for help. Let us now pray quietly and bring him our problems, troubles and worries.

Celebrant Lord God our Father, your people wait in joyful hope for the coming of your Son. May their preparation in this Advent season enable them to enter fully into the joy of Christmas. We ask this through Jesus Christ your Son, our Lord.

CHRISTMAS: MIDDAY MASS

Celebrant Today we celebrate the feast of the coming of our Saviour. Let us pray that the light of the world may continue to guide men's hearts and minds.

Reader We pray that the Church's Christmas joy will inspire it to guide mankind to a greater knowledge of Christ's redeeming love.
Lord, hear us. **Lord, graciously hear us.**

We pray for a renewed commitment to faith on the part of Christians, so that they may always follow Christ's guiding light.
Lord, hear us. **Lord, graciously hear us.**

For those who have not yet seen the light of Christ

For those who are not free to follow Christ as they would wish

For those who cannot recognise and accept the truth

Mary held the infant Jesus in her arms, so we join our prayers to hers. **Hail Mary...**

Let us pause to pray to our Saviour in silence.

Celebrant Lord God our Father, you have today sent your Son to be the light of the world. We pray that this light may shine in all corners of the earth where it has not yet reached, and that we may help carry this light, through Christ our Lord.

(Prayers for Midnight Mass are on p. 55, and for the Dawn Mass on p. 118.)

HOLY FAMILY

(1st Sunday after Christmas)

Celebrant On the feast of the Holy Family let us pray to God, our Father, for the needs of the human family everywhere.

Reader We pray first for peace in family life and for those who have been orphaned or widowed, that they may find comfort in God's love.

Let us pray to the Lord. **Draw all men to yourself, Lord.**

We pray for those whose hopes for marriage or for a family have not been fulfilled, that they may find peace in God's love.

Let us pray to the Lord. **Draw all men to yourself, Lord.**

For the newly married, for engaged couples, and for those in love

For foster parents and their children

For the housebound and those who care for them

Let us ask Mary, the wife of Joseph and mother of Jesus, to add her prayers to ours. **Hail Mary...**

Let us pray in silence for our own family and friends.

Celebrant God, our Father, you have made us your adopted sons and daughters; give us the grace to live as true children of your family. We make our prayer through Christ our Lord.

THE OCTAVE OF CHRISTMAS

The Solemnity of Mary, Mother of God

Celebrant As week ago we celebrated the birth of Jesus. Today we think especially of Mary his mother, whom he gave to us to be our mother and helper, and we pray with her for all mankind.

Reader For a spirit of fellowship among Christians, that all may be reconciled to their brothers and sisters and so be able to call God Father, we pray to the Lord.
Lord, in your mercy. **Hear our prayer**

For all parents, that they may learn humility and acceptance from Mary, and patience and understanding from Joseph, we pray to the Lord.
Lord, in your mercy. **Hear our prayer.**

For religious sisters, who exercise a spiritual motherhood

For our own mothers, whether alive or dead

For the Church, and all who work for the kingdom of God

Let us greet Mary, whom all generations have called blessed, with the words. **Hail Mary...**

Mary pondered in her heart all that happened to her. Love can speak without words, so let us be still for a short time in God's presence.

Celebrant Father, you made Mary an example to all mankind when she accepted the words of your messenger. May we ponder your words and be as willing to accept your messengers today, through your Son, Jesus Christ our Lord.

2nd SUNDAY AFTER CHRISTMAS

Celebrant We can know God only through Jesus, who was born into our world and lived a human life. Let us pray that by the light of Jesus mankind may grow in knowledge of God.

Reader We pray that the Spirit may remain with God's people, the Church, that it may stay ever faithful to the message of his Son.

We pray to the Lord. **Lord, hear our prayer**

We pray that the work of spreading the Gospel may prosper, so that the whole world will come to acknowledge the Son of God as Lord of all.

We pray to the Lord. **Lord, hear our prayer.**

For those who rule nations, that his Spirit may enter into their hearts

For the bishops, that they may work together

That Christians may witness to Jesus by their lives

Let us ask Mary, Jesus' mother, to present our prayers to her Son. **Hail Mary...**

Let us pray silently for what we need.

Celebrant God our Father, unite all those who bear the name of Christian, that the world may believe in Jesus Christ whom you have sent.

THE EPIPHANY

Celebrant Today we celebrate the revelation of the Son of God to the whole world. Let us pray that people everywhere will come to recognise him.

Reader Let us pray for the Church of Christ, that it may demonstrate its fidelity to Jesus by seeing him in the poor and the needy and by working for their salvation.
Come, Lord Jesus. **Come, Lord Jesus, come.**

Let us pray for missionaries in their work of spreading the Gospel, that they may be rewarded by seeing knowledge of Christ brought to all mankind.
Come, Lord Jesus. **Come, Lord Jesus, come.**

For statesmen and diplomats, that they may seek justice in international relations

For those who work in industry, that they may work for justice in industrial relations

For those in public life, that they may not compromise Christian principles

Let us ask Mary, who took Jesus to the Temple, to show him to us in the Church today. **Hail Mary...**

Let us pray in silence that Jesus may be revealed to us.

Celebrant Father, you have given us the gift of your Son. May his work among us continue in the power of the Holy Spirit. We make our prayer in his name, Jesus the Lord.

ASH WEDNESDAY

Celebrant The Church today begins a period for prayer and penance. Let us ask God to help Christians use it wisely.

Reader We pray for tranquility in this busy world, so that people everywhere may have time to listen to God and discover his will.
Lord, hear us. **Lord, graciously hear us.**

We pray for a spirit of generosity in dealings among nations, so that those who have nothing may gain the means of finding God.
Lord, hear us. **Lord, graciously hear us.**

We pray for a spirit of restraint in our own society, so that what it can produce may be fairly shared.
Lord, hear us. **Lord, graciously hear us.**

For the Pope and the bishops, who are Christ's special ambassadors

For handicapped people, who are Christ's special friends

Let us share our time of prayer with Mary, the mother of our Saviour. **Hail Mary...**

We must spend time in the desert if we are to know God. Let us be with him now in silence.

Celebrant Father, your Son was led by the Spirit into the desert. We pray that we may be led by the same Spirit to watch and to pray, so that we may not enter into temptation. We make our prayer through Christ Jesus our Lord.

1st SUNDAY OF LENT

Celebrant God watches over the world from day to day. So let us ask him` with confidence to listen to our prayers, for the Church and all mankind.

Reader Let us pray that Christ's Church may remain pure in act as well as in intention, and not be tempted to compromise with principalities and powers.
Lord, be with your people. **And hear our prayer.**

Let us pray that a spirit of toleration will spread through the world, that distinctions on grounds of colour, class and creed may vanish.
Lord, be with your people. **And hear our prayer.**

For statesmen, that they may speak and act with integrity

For the victims of prejudice, that they may find true friendship

For those who are searching for the truth, that they may find help

Let us ask Mary, the woman of faith, to add her prayers to ours. **Hail Mary...**

Let us pray for a moment in silence.

Celebrant Father, we need your grace especially when we are faced with temptation to compromise. Help us to grow more like your Son Jesus, who lives and reigns for ever.

2nd SUNDAY OF LENT

Celebrant The Lord is our light and our help, and there is no one we need fear. He invites us to put our trust in him and to ask for his gifts on behalf of all mankind.

Reader We pray that Christians in this busy world may learn to set aside time to be with Jesus, so that they may learn that it is good for them to be here.
In your mercy, Lord. **Hear our prayer.**

We pray that those who have taken up their cross to follow the Lord may persevere to the end of their journey.
In your mercy, Lord. **Hear our prayer.**

For those who are blind to God's glory

For those whose faith is weak

For those who have to work on Sundays

We ask Mary, who walked with her Son the road to Calvary, to stay with us on our journey. **Hail Mary...**

As the Apostles needed a quiet time with Jesus to see him as he really was, let us be with him a moment in silent prayer.

Celebrant Almighty God, the Apostles saw your Son transfigured by your glory. May your people be changed into a closer likeness of him, so that the world may see your glory. Through Christ our Lord.

3rd SUNDAY OF LENT

Celebrant The gospel calls us to conversion. Secure in the knowledge that our prayers are answered, let us pray for the conversion of the world.

Reader We pray for all those who have been special talents, that they may use them in the service of God for the good of their fellow men and women.

We pray to the Lord. **Lord, hear and answer our prayer.**

We pray for all those who work in education, that they may help the world to come to know God.

We pray to the Lord. **Lord, hear and answer our prayer.**

For those who work in the background, without hope of reward

For those who are preparing for marriage

For those who cannot yet forgive themselves

Mary trusted God completely. As we pray with her let us ask for a share of this trust. **Hail Mary...**

Now let us pray in silence.

Celebrant Almighty God, you are slow to anger and rich in mercy, so we come to you with great confidence, certain of your forgiving love, through Christ our Lord.

4th SUNDAY OF LENT

Celebrant We are ambassadors for Christ. With these words of St Paul in mind let us pray together for all God's people.

Reader We pray for Christians of every denomination, that they may be Christ's followers in deed and not merely in name.
Lord, hear us. **Lord, graciously hear us.**

We pray for all who like the prodigal son return to the fold. May they always find willing acceptance and forgiveness.
Lord, hear us. **Lord, graciously hear us.**

For leaders of different Christian Churches and bodies, that they may come to a better understanding

For those who find it hard to control their anger

For those who have quarrelled with menbers of their family

Let us ask Mary to help us to a deeper understanding of Christ's Passion. **Hail Mary...**

Let us pray in silence for those we have remembered.

Celebrant Lord God our Father, you have given us in the words of Christ the assurance that the penitent will find in you a loving father. May your people who have sinned be converted and live with you in your kingdom, through Christ our Lord.

5th SUNDAY OF LENT

Celebrant Man cannot live by bread alone, and so we ask God to sustain his people with his Spirit.

Reader Let us pray for the priests of Christ's Church, that they may faithfully break the living bread, preach the living word, and inspire a living faith.
We pray to you, Lord. **Lord, hear our prayer.**

Let us pray for the governments of nations, that they may get their priorities right and so enable the Spirit to work in the world.
We pray to you, Lord. **Lord, hear our prayer.**

For the hungry, that the Lenten fast may remind Christians of their plight

For those tempted to despair, that they may not lose hope

For people to rise above the letter of the law and accept its spirit

At the foot of the cross stood Mary the mother of Jesus. We now ask her to pray with us. **Hail Mary...**

In a few moments of silence we remember those who have asked us to pray for them.

Celebrant Father, when our spirit is unwilling and our flesh is weak, strengthen us with the power of your Spirit, through Christ our Lord.

6th SUNDAY OF LENT

Passion Sunday

Celebrant The spirit is willing, but the flesh is weak. Let us pray that we may not be put to the test, and say: Father, your will be done.

Reader We pray for those who are in an agony of fear, or of sickness.
Let us pray. **Father, your will be done.**

We pray for all Christian Churches, that through the suffering of disunity there may grow a rich union under Christ.
Let us pray. **Father, your will be done.**

For those who witness to their faith in an alien world

For those who still make Jerusalem a battle-ground

For those who stir up crowds to hatred

Mary was promised that a sword would pierce her heart. We ask her to pray compassionately with us. **Hail Mary...**

It is in silence that the Word may be most clearly heard. So let us now listen in our hearts.

Celebrant Almighty Father, we are willing servants, but are often slow to walk with your Son. We know that there is no easy path to happiness, and we pray for the perseverance and strength to drink the cup of suffering, which we are to share with your Son, Jesus Christ.

MAUNDY THURSDAY

Celebrant Our Lord and Master became the sacrificial Lamb, who lived and died for others. Let us pray that men will live and die following this example. So with him we pray: Father, your will be done.

Reader We pray for the whole Church, the living Body of Christ. May the members of this Body always be willing to give themselves generously for the world.
We pray with Christ. **Father, your will be done.**

We pray for the Jewish people, against whom Christians have sinned. May they come to a fulfilment of their hopes through Jesus, the Saviour of the world.
We pray with Christ. **Father, your will be done.**

For those in the agony of a breakdown, that they may find support and encouragement

For the gift of humility, and for those who have found the lowest place

For priests, that they may offer Mass with conviction, and live it in their lives

Tonight, recalling Mary's pain as she prayed for her Son at the hour of his death we ask her to pray with us.
Hail Mary...

Let us pray in silence that we may not be put to the test.

Celebrant Father, you have given us in Jesus an example of perfect love. Teach us this sacrificial love so that nothing will separate us from him who lives with you now and always.

EASTER SUNDAY

Celebrant Let us pray to God, the almighty Father, who raised his Son Jesus from the dead. Let us ask him that all his people may share in the glory of the resurrection.

Reader Let us pray for Christians throughout the world. May they remain true to the new life they received at baptism and live always with the life of the risen Christ.
Lord, in your mercy. **Hear our prayer.**

Let us pray for all those who this Easter have received new life by baptism. May they discover the face of the risen Christ in their new brothers and sisters in the Lord.
Lord, in your mercy. **Hear our prayer.**

For the spread of the Gospel among those who know nothing of the resurrection

For the sick and dying whom Christ invites in a special way to share in his sufferings so as to share in his resurrection

For the Church, that its faith in the resurrection may be strengthened

Let us pray to Mary, who was filled with joy at her Son's being raised from the dead. **Hail Mary...**

Let us contemplate the risen Christ in silence.

Celebrant Father, it is because of your Son's death and resurrection, and the power of the Holy Spirit, that our prayers are surely heard by you. Guide us today that we may be found worthy to share the resurrection of your Son, who lives and reigns for ever.

2nd SUNDAY OF EASTER

Celebrant Christ is the beginning and the end of all things, the first-born of all creation and he to whom all honour and glory belong. We pray now to the Father, in the name of his Son and filled with his Spirit, for the needs of the world.

Reader We pray that people will come to believe in the risen Lord, even though they have not seen him, so that his work will spread.
We pray to you, Lord. **Lord, hear our prayer.**

We pray that Christians may learn to forgive each other and so show the world the work of the Spirit.
We pray to you, Lord. **Lord, hear our prayer.**

For the outcasts of society, that they may find true friendship

For those who are beginning their last term at school or college

For those who do unpleasant jobs

Let us ask the holy mother of our saviour to pray with us.
Hail Mary...

Now let us pray quietly for a few moments with faith in the Lord.

Celebrant God our Father, your risen Son is the new creation. We pray that we and all mankind may make this new creation the centre of their lives so as to share the life of your kingdom, where he lives with you and the Spirit for ever.

3rd SUNDAY OF EASTER

Celebrant Conscious that the risen Christ is concerned for the needs of all mankind, we pray to the Father in his name.

Reader Let us pray for the Church of Christ, that all its members, transformed by the new life of the risen Lord, may go out with confidence to meet Jesus in their fellow men and women.

Lord, hear us. **Lord, graciously hear us.**

Let us pray for those who have to preach the Gospel in an atmosphere of hostility or indifference, that their words may be heard.

Lord, hear us. **Lord, graciously hear us.**

For those who work on the sea: fishermen, seamen, divers

For those with power over the freedom of others: judges, magistrates, immigration officials, police.

For artists, sculptors, poets, who help us see the beauty of life more deeply

Let us ask Mary, who knew the joy of the resurrection, to pray with us as we say: **Hail Mary...**

Let us offer our own prayers in the silence of our hearts.

Celebrant Father, you have given your people new life in the risen Lord. May the Spirit enable us all today to live as new men and women so that your kingdom will come, through Christ our Lord.

4th SUNDAY OF EASTER

Celebrant Christ, the Good Shepherd, is our leader and guide. Let us pray that his people may learn to accept his leadership, and so come to the Father.

Reader Let us pray for all members of the Church: bishops, priests, religious and lay people, that they may willingly accept their responsibilities and work together.
Lord, hear our prayer. **And let our cry come to you.**

Let us pray that the Church may recognise suitable candidates for the priesthood and the religious life. We pray that these men and women may have the courage to do all that their vocation calls them to do.
Lord, hear our prayer. **And let our cry come to you.**

For national leaders and governments

For those who work in food production

For all those with special responsibilites in our parish

Let us ask Mary, the mother of the Good Shepherd, to pray for us. **Hail Mary...**

Let us pray in silence.

Celebrant Heavenly Father, fill your people with the spirit of joy, that they may follow Christ, the Good Shepherd, to eternal life. We ask this in his name.

5th SUNDAY OF EASTER

Celebrant God holds the whole world in his hands, and his Spirit renews the face of the earth. Let us pray that this work of renewal may continue in the Church and the world.

Reader That Christians may give an example of Christ to the rest of humanity by loving one another as Christ loved his friends — and his enemies —, we pray to the Lord.
Lord, hear us. **Lord, hear our prayer.**

That the Spirit of God working in his people may bring comfort and consolation wherever there is sadness and mourning, we pray to the Lord.
Lord, hear us. **Lord, hear our prayer.**

For doctors and midwives who help to bring new life into the world

For those with dangerous and unglamorous jobs

For those who have lost interest in other people

Mary gave a wonderful example of love; let us ask for her prayers. **Hail Mary...**

Let us pray silently for a renewal of the Spirit within us.

Celebrant Father, your love is gracious and without end. We pray that your people may respond to your grace with generosity, through Christ our Lord.

6th SUNDAY OF EASTER

Celebrant The risen Christ has sent us his Spirit so that we might be God's partners in the salvation of the world. With this in mind, let us pray.

Reader That Christians may become more aware of the presence of the Spirit in their daily life, and be open to his influence in their choices.
Lord, hear us. **Lord, graciously hear us.**

That all who work for the destitute may persevere in their labours, and spread the peace of Christ.
Lord, hear us. **Lord, graciously hear us.**

For those whose faith is tested by persecution or doubt

For those who try to be peacemakers at work and at home

For those who find it hard to accept the truth

We ask our Lady to help mankind find the way, the means and the strength to live in the way of her Son.
Hail Mary...

Let us pray quietly for a moment.

Celebrant Lord God, we pray that your people may receive the gift of your Spirit with eagerness, and so help to refresh the world. We make our prayer through Christ our Lord.

ASCENSION DAY

Celebrant Jesus went from this world that his Spirit might continue to guide the Church. Conscious of his continued presence in us through the Spirit, let us pray for the Church and for all mankind.

Reader May the Spirit of the Lord, working with the apostles after the Ascension, continue to help his Church to make disciples of all nations.
We pray to the Lord. **Lord, hear our prayer.**

May the Spirit of Christ be especially with those who have been baptised this Easter, that they in turn may one day go out and preach everywhere.
We pray to the Lord. **Lord, hear our prayer.**

For the civil authorities, that they may recognize the authority of Christ

For those trying to believe in themselves, and those trying to believe in something greater than themselves

For those who are despondent and have little hope

Because Mary is in heaven with Christ, she is with us. Let us ask her to pray for us. **Hail Mary...**

Now in silent prayer we gladly welcome the hope and promise that this feast day brings us.

Celebrant Father, with your Son enthroned in glory, you send us the gift of your Spirit. May that Spirit fill us with joy and hope as we play our part in building up your kingdom, through Christ our Lord.

7th SUNDAY OF EASTER

Celebrant The Spirit invites all those who are thirsty to come so that they may receive the water of life. Let us then pray to the Lord for he is good, and his mercy is without end.

Reader Let us pray for unity in our homes, where we work, among Christians and among all people of good will, so that the world may believe that the Lord is with us.
Come, Lord Jesus. **Come, Lord Jesus, come.**

Let us pray that there will always be men and women like St Stephen the first martyr, ready and willing to declare their faith even to death.
Come, Lord Jesus. **Come, Lord Jesus, come.**

For those who reject the water of life

For Samaritans and others who care for those in need

For people whose security has been shattered by change

Let us pray with Mary that the Spirit may overshadow us.
Hail Mary...

Now in quietness let us pray to God in his goodness and mercy.

Celebrant Lord God our Father, you send your Spirit to be our refreshment and our hope. May your people always respond to the gift of the Spirit by serving others as they were taught to do by Jesus Christ, your Son, our Lord.

PENTECOST SUNDAY

Celebrant The Spirit of God came to the apostles so that they could speak to the world about the wonderful works of God. Let us pray for that Spirit to be with his people as they are sent out into the world.

Reader Let us pray for the Church, that all the gifts of the Spirit may work in its members, and that they may recognize the different gifts in one another.
Come Holy Spirit. **Fill the hearts of your faithful.**

Let us pray for all men and women, that the love, patience, kindness and gentleness of the Spirit may rule their hearts and deeds.
Come Holy Spirit. **Fill the hearts of your faithful.**

For those who are not at peace with themselves or their fellow men

For families and friends who have quarrelled

For non-Christians who are searching for God's Spirit

Let us pray that like Mary we may be obedient to the Spirit. **Hail Mary...**

God's Spirit is in our hearts; let us be still and know him.

Celebrant Lord God, you have shown yourself in the power and warmth of your Spirit. As your people go into the world to do your will send them your Spirit that they may walk with confidence and humility. We make our prayer through Christ our Lord.

CORPUS CHRISTI

Celebrant Jesus is the Bread of Life. Let us pray that his life may continue to nourish the Church and the world.

Reader We pray that all men and women will come to know Christ in his followers by the sign of breaking of bread and the fact of sharing of life.
Bread of Life. **Hear our prayer.**

We pray that the Church will share the spirit of Christ's sacrifice as it shares his body and blood, and be an instrument of service to the world.
Bread of Life. **Hear our prayer.**

For the hungry, that they receive their fair share

For those who find it hard to believe in the Real Presence

For the sick and aged unable to come to Mass with the rest of the parish

Let us pray with Mary, the mother of Jesus, who gave us her Son. **Hail Mary...**

Let us pray quietly for a moment.

Celebrant Lord God our Father, your Son fed the five thousand with bread brought to him. As we bring him the bread of our daily work, may he give us back the bread of eternal life. We make this prayer in his name, Jesus Christ our Lord.

TRINITY SUNDAY

Celebrant Today we worship God as three-in-one: Father, Son and Holy Spirit. So we make our prayers to the Father through the Son for all his people whom he gathers together in his Spirit.

Reader May Christ's Church on earth, guided by the Word of God and inspired by his Spirit, be a beacon of light to the world.
Lord, hear our prayer. **And let our cry come to you.**

May all who share the baptism of the Lord, come also to share the one Bread. May the Holy Spirit help us to grow in unity.
Lord, hear our prayer. **And let our cry come to you.**

For those who have recently been confirmed

For those who are cut off from the Eucharist

For the sick and handicapped in the parish

Let us ask Mary, the Mother of God, to pray for us.
Hail Mary...

Let us now silently open our hearts to the Spirit in peace and confidence.

Celebrant God our Father, you gave your Son to be our truth and our guidance. May his presence in the Eucharist and the power of his Spirit in our hearts give us renewed confidence in your unfailing love.

THE SACRED HEART

Celebrant Today's feast reminds us of the love of God for all his children. This gives us the confidence to open our hearts and pray for the needs of mankind.

Reader As the good shepherd went after the lost sheep, may Christians always remember those in need and never close their hearts to them.
In your mercy, Lord. **Hear our prayer.**

Let us pray that those who believe in the Father may remain strong in their belief through the Son who poured out his love for them.
In your mercy, Lord. **Hear our prayer.**

For those who have lost their way and sense of meaning in life

For those who know they are dying

For those who fail to see the many signs God gives us for his love and concern for us

We ask Mary, who was so close to Jesus, to pray for us.
Hail Mary...

Let us now open our hearts to God in our own silent prayer.

Celebrant God our Father, you loved the world so much that you sent your Son, who poured out his blood that the world might be saved. Hear the prayers we make to you in his name, that his love in us may never fail.

THE PRESENTATION

(February 2)

Celebrant Lord, you have prepared a light to enlighten all mankind. May this light guide us in our prayers for the needs of this community and of the whole world.

Reader We ask on this day a blessing on all mothers, that they may be as true to God's will as was Mary.
We pray to the Lord. **He is our light and our salvation.**

We pray for a greater eagerness in preaching the Gospel, and a stronger faith, so that all men may come to see the light of the world.
We pray to the Lord. **He is our light and our salvation.**

For those who are called to serve God as unmarried people

For those who work unsocial hours

For prisoners of conscience

Like Simeon we pray that we might see our saviour. We ask Mary to show us the way to him. **Hail Mary...**

Let us pray in silence as we offer ourselves to God.

Celebrant Father, we pray that Christians may be lights to the world so that others may know you. We make our prayer through Christ who is the light for all ages, now and for ever.

ST JOSEPH

(March 19)

Celebrant St Joseph is shown to us in the gospels as fair-minded, patient and understanding. Let us ask that Christians today may take his example to heart as we pray for the needs of mankind.

Reader Let us pray for the Church, that its work for the salvation of the world may be carried on with patience and concern for justice.
We pray to the Lord. **Lord, hear our prayer.**

Let us pray for all who exercise a fatherly authority, both in their families and at work. May their concern and example be such as to reflect the qualities of St Joseph and the fatherhod of God.
We pray to the Lord. **Lord, hear our prayer.**

For those who work by the skill of their hands

For those who are unemployed

For families in difficulties: the homeless, the poor, the one-parent families

Mary could not have accepted God's invitation unless she had the consent, support and understanding of her husband. With confidence we invite her to pray with us. **Hail Mary...**

Like St Joseph let us consider in silence the marvels of God's love.

Celebrant Father, you gave us the example of Joseph to inspire our family and working lives. May your people follow his example and so help to make the presence of your Son grow in the world today. We ask this through Christ your Son.

THE ANNUNCIATION

(March 25)

Celebrant The announcement of the Lord's birth was the beginning of the good news which Christians are called on to proclaim. Let us ask the Father, in Jesus's name, that they may bear witness to the Gospel, and announce to the men and women of our own time that God is with us.

Reader Let us pray that all Christians will be as willing as Mary to listen carefully to the messages God sends them and to act according to his will.
Lord, in your mercy. **Hear our prayer.**

Let us pray that the message of hope and joy proclaimed in today's feast may penetrate this troubled world through the agency of the Church of Christ.
Lord, in your mercy. **Hear our prayer.**

For all who work to spread the good news

For those who are searching but have not found

For those who are bitter and are deaf to words of forgiveness

Encouraged by Mary's faithful response to the message she recevied from God let us ask her help. **Hail Mary...**

Let us pause silently and pray to the Lord in the stillness of our hearts.

Celebrant Lord God, in times past you spoke through the prophets, now you speak through Christ your Son. As they receive the good news of his coming with joy, help your people now to announce his Gospel with boldness and deep conviction for the spread of your kingdom. We ask this through the same Christ our Lord.

SS JOHN FISHER & THOMAS MORE

(June 22)

Celebrant St John Fisher and St Thomas Moore are two great saints of the English Church. Let us pray for the needs of the Church in our own land and throughout the world.

Reader We pray that the example of the lives and deaths of St John Fisher and St Thomas More may inspire the Christians of this land to stand up for what they know to be right.
Lord, hear us. **Lord graciously hear us.**

We pray that the holiness and courage shown by these two great saints may be an example to those in public office, that they may respect individual freedom while working for the good of the community.
Lord, hear us. **Lord graciously hear us.**

For all those working to heal the wounds left by the Reformation

For all who suffer in their fight for truth and liberty under totalitarian regimes

For all those in doubt

England was once known as Mary's dowry, so let us ask her to add her prayers to ours as we say. **Hail Mary...**

In a spirit of faith let us pray in silence.

Celebrant (A prayer of St Thomas More)
Make us all, good Lord, virtually participant of your holy sacrament this day, and every day make us lively members, sweet Saviour Christ, of your holy Mystical Body, your Catholic Church. We make our prayer through Christ, our Lord.

ST JOHN THE BAPTIST

(June 24)

Celebrant The message of John the Baptist was that repentance should produce the appropriate fruits: sharing, giving, fairness to others. Let us pray that his message may be heard and acted on in the Church and the world today.

Reader We pray for all Christians, that they may not rely on what they have learnt for salvation but through their deeds produce their own good fruit.
Lord, hear our prayer. **And grant us your salvation.**

We pray for those in goverment and the civil service, that they may deal with citizens in fairness, not exacting more than their rate; and for those in the armed forces, that they may defend freedom and not uphold tyranny.
Lord, hear our prayer. **And grant us your salvation.**

For those who are unrepentant, that their hearts may be touched

For those who have recently been baptized

For those who have recently been received into the Church

As Mary's Son was baptized by John, let us ask her to help us remain faithful to our baptismal promises. **Hail Mary...**

We pray in silence, remembering our baptismal vows.

Celebrant Lord God our Father, you showed youself to your Son at the moment of his baptism by John. May all who follow in his footsteps come to know your will, through the same Jesus Christ your Son, our Lord.

SS PETER & PAUL

(June 29)

Celebrant Jesus entrusted his Church to the leadership of the apostles. On the feast of St Peter and St Paul, let us ask the risen Lord to send his Spirit on his present-day apostles.

Reader Let us pray for our Pope and for all who are called to the service of responsibility and authority in the Church. May they recognise their weaknesses, and rely on the strength of the true Rock who is Christ.
We pray to the Lord. **Lord, hear our prayer.**

Let us pray for all those in authority in the world and for all those who work in the communications media. May the former work with the integrity and devotion of St Peter and the latter with the clarity and zeal of St Paul.
We pray to the Lord. **Lord, hear our prayer.**

For charity, understanding, a sense of proportion and humour, when groups of Christians disagree

For an apostolic spirit in the Church, looking outward to the whole of humanity.

For courage and integrity, that the Church and its members may speak the truth in love

Let us ask Mary to join us in our prayers that all Christians may share the spirit of these two pillars of the Church. **Hail Mary...**

Let us pray in silence for the needs of the Church and of the world.

Celebrant Lord God our Father, you sent your Son to save the world through the work of your Church. May the example of the steadfast Peter and of Paul who fought the good fight inspire your people today to keep and proclaim the faith that comes to us from the apostles. Through Christ our Lord.

THE TRANSFIGURATION

(August 6)

Celebrant Peter, James and John, the three close friends of Jesus, were given a glimpse of the transfigured Christ, glorious and majestic. Faith enables us, too, to come close to the risen Christ. Let us pray to him for the needs of the world.

Reader We pray for the Church of Christ, that like the apostles Jesus took with him, it may come to see the glory of Christ in his humanity, and recognize him in the poor and needy today.
We pray to the Lord. **Lord, hear our prayer.**

We pray for all those who do not know Christ. May they follow the light of their consciences and so come to share in a reflection of his glory.
We pray to the Lord. **Lord, hear our prayer.**

For the Pope, shepherd of the Church, that he may enjoy confident faith and hope

For those in love, that they may transfigure one another

For all who need a transfiguration in their lives

We ask Mary who lived by faith and now shares the glory of her Son, to take our prayers to him. **Hail Mary...**

Let us pray silently for what we need.

Celebrant Father, your Son was transfigured for the apostles who looked on him with love and understanding. May we his people look on him with the same love and not put any obstacles in the way of the full manifestation of God. We ask this through Christ our Lord.

THE ASSUMPTION OF OUR LADY

(August 15)

Celebrant Mary showed absolute acceptance of God's will, and so all generations call her blessed. In the knowledge that because she is in heaven, she is with us, let us pray for the needs of the Church and the world.

Reader We pray that the whole Church will mirror the faithfulness of Mary, saying with her: Behold the handmaid of the Lord, be it done to be according to your will.
Lord, hear us. **Lord, graciously hear us.**

We pray that in the search for Christian unity, our Lady will not be a stumbling block, but a sign of hope.
Lord, hear us. **Lord, graciously hear us.**

For those who look for guidance in family relationships

For the homeless

For those caring for and loving their disturbed or handicapped children

Mary could rightly say: 'The Lord has done marvels for me'. We ask her help and prayers. **Hail Mary...**

In a few precious moments of silence we open our hearts to God.

Celebrant Lord God, you gave Mary the strength to stand beneath the cross of Jesus, and you filled her with joy at his resurrection. May we share her strength and come to share her present glory, through Christ our Lord.

THE EXALTATION OF THE HOLY CROSS

(September 14)

Celebrant As we celebrate the loving wisdom and the mercy of our God, by whom the Cross of Calvary is made for us the Tree of Life, let us pray for all mankind.

Reader Let us pray for those who in their sufferings are most like Jesus: the poor, the lonely, the rejected, the oppressed, that they may be brought through their cross to the joy of the resurrection.
Lord, we pray. **Save us by your holy cross.**

Let us pray for those who make for themselves a God with the attributes they would like to possess: power, riches, success. May they be converted by looking at God suffering and dying on a cross.
Lord, we pray. **Save us by your holy cross.**

For those who hang upon the cross of sickness or despair

That people may come to see the cross as a sign of forgiveness and rebirth

That Christians may become more aware that sin harms the whole Body of Christ

We turn to her who learned the cost of being Christ's disciple as she stood beside his cross. **Hail Mary...**

Now we pray in silence to the Father who gave us his Son that we might learn to give ourselves.

Celebrant Father, you so loved the world that you gave your only Son to save mankind. Make firm and strong our faith in him that by his wounds we may be healed and through his Cross may come to life. We make our prayers in his name, Jesus the Lord.

ALL SAINTS

(November 1)

Celebrant We believe that we are one people, and that every person of every nation, race, tribe and language is a child of God. As one people let us now turn to God in prayer.

Reader Let us pray for all who show an example of holiness to the world. May they lead all men and women to the kingdom God has reserved for those whom he loves.
Lord, in your mercy. **Hear our prayer.**

Let us pray for all those who try to follow the law of love and fail. May they find help and support and so come to enjoy the company of the saints.
Lord, in your mercy. **Hear our prayer.**

For those who are persecuted in the name of Christ

For those who are sick and dying

For those who believe differently from us

Mary is queen of heaven and our mother. Let us ask her to pray for us. **Hail Mary...**

With the whole company of saints, let us pray in our hearts.

Celebrant Father of all mankind, draw us together into one people under the outstretched arms of your Son, so that filled with your Spirit we may praise you now and always.

THE IMMACULATE CONCEPTION

(December 8)

Celebrant God chose Mary to be the mother of our Saviour and kept her free from sin. On her feast day let us pray for all men and women, brothers and sisters in Christ.

Reader Let us pray that through the example of Mary, the virtue of chastity may be understood and practised by all as a work of love and fulfilment.
Lord of life hear us. **Lord hear us.**

Let us pray for mothers of families, that they may grow in generosity, in practical charity, in gentleness and in patience.
Lord of life hear us. **Lord hear us.**

For young people in today's world

For those who practise celibacy for the sake of God's kingdom

For those who find their vocation hard

In Mary there was no stain of sin. Let us ask for the help of her prayers. **Hail Mary...**

Mary kept things in her heart. Let us, like her, pray for a moment in silence.

Celebrant Lord God our Father, you gave Mary to the world as an example of wholeness and acceptance. May her love help us to see and accept your will. We ask this in the name of her Son, Jesus Christ our Lord.

THE SACRAMENT OF BAPTISM

Celebrant Dear fellow Christians, as members of God's family we are here to welcome N. into our community. God our Father is present with us now, as he was present at the baptism of his Son Jesus in the river Jordan. So we look to him with trust, asking his help for all Christians, and especially for the new member of this world-wide family.

Reader We pray for N. whom we welcome into the Church today. May he/she grow in faith and love, and so become a light to the world.
Lord, hear us. **Lord, graciously hear us.**

We pray for the parents (and friends) of N. who have shared their faith with their child (friend). May their example help this child of God grow in knowledge and love.
Lord, hear us. **Lord, graciously hear us.**

We pray for the godparents of N., who have undertaken to guide him/her in growth in faith. May their own faith remain firm, and may they find their task a rewarding one.
Lord, hear us. **Lord, graciously hear us.**

We pray for all mothers and fathers, that when their children's faith is weak theirs may be strong. May they never lose hope.
Lord, hear us. **Lord, graciously hear us.**

We pray for those who do not know Christ, for those who are searching for a meaning to life, and for those who are thirsty for God's Spirit.
Lord, hear us. **Lord, graciously hear us.**

Let us pray to Mary, who guided her Son to manhood. **Hail Mary...**

For a moment let us listen to God's Spirit in our hearts.

Celebrant God our Father, we wish to work with you in sharing your light and truth with our families and friends. May we be always faithful to this task. We make our prayer through Christ our Lord.

THE RECEPTION OF A CONVERT

Celebrant In our great joy at receiving our brother/sister into the full communion of the Church, let us pray together.

Reader For N., that he/she may grow ever more into the likeness of the living Christ.
We pray to the Lord. **Lord, hear us.**

For all who are gathered here to share his/her happiness, that our own faith may not fail.
We pray to the Lord. **Lord, hear us.**

For those who first awakened the gift of faith in N. and for those who instructed him/her in the teachings of the Church.
We pray to the Lord. **Lord, hear us.**

For our brethren of other Christian Churches. Under the guidance of the Spirit, may we all be drawn into a common fellowship and a united worship.
We pray to the Lord. **Lord, hear us.**

For those of little faith, for those seeking the truth, and for those in despair.
We pray to the Lord. **Lord, hear us.**

Let us pray to Mary, the mother of all those who have found new life in Christ. **Hail Mary...**

In our new life, we need to pray in silence.

Celebrant Father, you have given us great joy in leading our friend into the full communion of your Church. Make us ever more aware of the goodness you show to us. We ask this through your Son, Jesus Christ our Lord.

FIRST COMMUNION

Celebrant We rejoice today with those who are receiving communion for the first time. In our joy, let us pray for them, for our parish community and for the wider community.

Reader Let us pray that these children may make their communion today with faith and joy in the Lord they are receiving.
Lord, hear us. **Lord, graciously hear us.**

We pray that as their awareness of what they are doing grows, so they may grow in faith and practice.
Lord, hear us. **Lord, graciously hear us.**

We pray that as today they welcome Jesus to their hearts, so they may always welcome others and be welcomed by others.
Lord, hear us. **Lord, graciously hear us.**

Let us pray for their parents, teachers and friends, that this occasion may lead all of us to a deeper faith in Christ's presence among us.
Lord, hear us. **Lord, graciously hear us.**

Let us pra for those in other parts of the world who are not free to worship, that they may be strengthened in faith, hope and love.
Lord, hear us. **Lord, graciously hear us.**

Let us ask Mary to join us in our prayer. **Hail Mary...**

Let us pray quietly for a moment.

Celebrant God our Father, you have invited us to know, love and serve you through your son, who comes to us as our spiritual food and drink. We pray that we may all grow into faithful disciples of your Son, Jesus Christ our Lord, who lives and reigns with you for ever and ever.

THE SACRAMENT OF CONFIRMATION

Celebrant On the occasion of this Confirmation we turn to God and pray for those who are being confirmed, for those they are joining in their mature faith, and for the needs of mankind.

Reader Let us pray for all those who are being confirmed today: may their strengthened faith be always a source of joy to them and a guide to their actions for the rest of their lives.
Lord, hear us. **Lord, graciously hear us.**

Let us pray for those other members of the community who have been confirmed. May this occasion confirm them in their faith.
Lord, hear us. **Lord, graciously hear us.**

Let us pray for those who work to bring peace to the world, that this may be seen by all as the work of the Spirit.
Lord, hear us. **Lord, graciously hear us.**

Let us pray for those who from birth, accident or old age, are dulled in mind or spirit, that they may have a special sense of belonging.
Lord, hear us. **Lord, graciously hear us.**

Let us pray for those who follow the ways of lies and of crime, that they may come to accept the spirit of truth in their lives.
Lord, hear us. **Lord, graciously hear us.**

Let us now turn to our blessed Lady, a source of strength and inspiration throughout the history of the Church, as we ask her protection and help. **Hail Mary...**

We now pray in silence that all may respond to the Spirit of Jesus in their lives.

Celebrant Heavenly Father, strengthen your people so that they may have the gifts of wisdom ad understanding, courage and love, and so serve you faithfully all their lives. We make this prayer through Christ our Lord.

THE SACRAMENT OF MARRIAGE

Celebrant Love one another as I have loved you. With these words of Jesus in mind we make our prayers today.

Reader For N. and N., that their lives will be filled with joy and peace, that their love will go from strength to strength, and that their deepest hopes on this day will come to fulfilment.
In your mercy, Lord. **Hear our prayer.**

For their parents, that having given them life in the beginning, they will with joy now see them build a new life together.
In your mercy, Lord. **Hear our prayer.**

For their families and friends; for those who give them care and support; for those who have encouraged them in their love for one another; for those they think of with gratitude today who are separated from them in life or by death.
In your mercy, Lord. **Hear our prayer.**

For those whose hopes for marriage have not yet been fulfilled; for those whose marriages have proved unhappy or impossible; for those who have lost a partner, a child, or a loved one.
In your mercy, Lord. **Hear our prayer.**

For those who by choice or circumstance remain single; for those who have embraced a life of celibacy or of virginity.
In your mercy, Lord. **Hear our prayer.**

Let us ask our Lady who interceded at the marriage feast in Cana, to pray with us at this marriage feast. **Hail Mary...**

In a few moments of silence let us pray for this new family and the family of man.

Celebrant Lord God, bring to completion in your own way and your own time the love which you have begun in each of us. Through Christ our Lord.

THE ANOINTING OF THE SICK

Celebrant We are together with our friends to pray for those who are sick. Let us pray that this anointing may give them an increase in faith, hope and love; assure them of forgiveness; and bring them to the fulness of life.

Reader We pray that through this anointing the Lord's love may strengthen those who are sick.
Put forth your hand, Lord. **And we shall be healed.**

May he who made the blind to see, the lame to walk and the deaf to hear, be with us in our prayers. We pray not for ourselves but for those who are in need.
Put forth your hand, Lord. **And we shall be healed.**

Let us pray for those who are close to death and who are afraid, that the Lord may give them peace and confidence.
Put forth your hand, Lord. **And we shall be healed.**

We pray for those who carry the cross of sickness daily, that they may learn patience and hope.
Put forth your hand, Lord. **And we shall be healed.**

Mary, the mother of sorrows, prays with us, now and at the hour of our suffering. **Hail Mary...**

Let us pray to God in silent hope.

Celebrant Father, we pray in faith for all those who are sick that they may be forgiven their sins, and so brought to a fulness of health and life. Through Christ our Lord.

A FUNERAL MASS

Celebrant At the conclusion of one earthly life, let us celebrate, though with sadness, the fact of eternal life with God. Let us pray to our ever loving Father.

Reader Let us pray for all here present, that our memory of N. whom we loved may inspire us with a renewed love for our fellow men and women.
In your mercy, Lord. **Hear our prayer.**

Let us ask God to forgive N. his/her sins and failings, confident that he/she will be welcomed by the whole communion of saints.
In your mercy, Lord. **Hear our prayer.**

Let us pray especially for the sorrowing relatives and friends, that the pain of their sorrow may be softened, and that the emptiness may be filled by the love of God.
In your mercy, Lord. **Hear our prayer.**

Let us pray for all those who are sick, and those who care for them, that they may grow in love and respect for each other.
In your mercy, Lord. **Hear our prayer.**

Mary was close to Jesus when he died, so we know that she can understand our sorrow at this time. Let us turn to her for help. **Hail Mary...**

Let us now pray in silence for the repose of the soul of our friend N.

Celebrant Heavenly Father, our time on earth passes quickly, we are like grass that grows, withers and dies. Support us as we travel towards you, and grant that we may all meet together again in your presence, with Christ Jesus our Lord.

A HARVEST FESTIVAL

Celebrant As we gather together to thank God for his continued goodness, let us pray for those through whom he has worked, for those less fortunate than ourselves, and for all mankind.

Reader We pray for farmers, farm workers, fishermen and all who have laboured to provide food from land and sea. May they feel joy in sharing in God's creation.
Let us pray. **Father, renew the face of the earth.**

We pray for scientists researching new and better ways to harvest the riches of the earth, so that the hungry may be fed.
Let us pray. **Father, renew the face of the earth.**

We pray that the dry lands of the world may receive help from other nations, so that the thirsty may be refreshed.
Let us pray. **Father, renew the face of the earth.**

We pray for the work of all agencies that promote the growth of food and its distribution throughout the world.
Let us pray. **Father, renew the face of the earth.**

We pray for those who waste the resources of the earth, who use living creatures unworthily. May they come to appreciate the oneness and dignity of God's creation.
Let us pray. **Father, renew the face of the earth.**

Let us pray with Mary, who gave her Son food, drink and shelter. **Hail Mary...**

In silence, let us remember the injustice of poverty in a world of plenty.

Celebrant Father, you have prepared a marriage feast for all nations. At Cana your Son ensured that there was enough for all. Work your wonders today, through us, so that the hungry may be fed. We ask this, like Mary, through your Son, Jesus Christ.